Shining the Boot of a Nation

A Portrait of Egypt after Nasser

Also by David Balderstone

A Road from Damascus

'Balderstone's novel is about people, land and displacement. It traces the lives of one-time Jerusalem friends and neighbours, the Palestinian Habeebs and the Jewish Avrahams as war, politics and ideology separate them, and then makes their paths cross again. Balderstone has the cadences and the speeches they enwrap just right too....above all he gets the people of the region right.'

The Age, Melbourne

The Baghdad Chameleon

'Like its predecessor, *A Road from Damascus,* this adventure is centred in the Middle East and sows a triangle of intrigue between Cyprus, Syria and Iraq.... When our Middle Eastern News diet is primarily pictures of violence and Islamic extremism, The Baghdad Chameleon provides the counter-image of complex interrelated cultures united by the pragmatism of doing deals.'

The Australian

DAVID BALDERSTONE

Shining the Boot of a Nation

A Portrait of Egypt after Nasser

THE
POPPY
PRESS
AUSTRALIA

© Susan Balderstone 2015

ISBN 978-0-9943464-2-1

All rights reserved. No part of this publication may be reproduced without the prior permission of the publisher and copyright owner except for brief excerpts for the purpose of fair criticism and comment acknowledging both author and publisher.

Cover photograph by Susan Balderstone
View of the Nile along Abu el Feda, Zamalek, Cairo in 1970

National Library of Australia
Cataloguing-in-Publication entry
Creator: Balderstone, David, author
Title: Shining the Boot of a Nation: A Portrait of Egypt after Nasser/ David Balderstone.
ISBN: 9780994346421 (paperback)
Subjects: Nasser, Gamal, Abdel, 1918-1970
        Egypt--Politics and government--1970-1981
        Egypt--History--1970-1981
        Egypt--Social life and customs
Dewey Number: 962.054

Published by
The Poppy Press AUSTRALIA
(Australian business name registration number 1064567K)
P.O.B. 850, Parkville, Victoria, 3052, Australia
Poppypress@bigpond.com

Contents

Foreword 3
Introduction 5
Map 6
1. A shoeshine in Abu el Feda Street. Sadat addresses the National Assembly 7
2. Events surrounding the death of President Nasser 18
3. Leadership manoeuvrings and the influence of Mohammed Heikal. Life in Abu el Feda 25
4. The Free Officers and the 1952 revolution 40
5. Sadat forms a government 45
6. Cairo life. Hassan the shoeshiner leaves for Luxor. A frozen peace initiative and build-up of arms 49
7. Hassan the shoeshiner arrives in Luxor. The end of forty days' mourning for Nasser 71
8. Ramadan in Abu el Feda. Attempts at Arab federation by Egypt, Sudan, Libya and Syria 79
9. Provocation along the Suez Canal and Egypt's diplomatic offensive. Bairam feast – the end of Ramadan in Abu el Feda 94
10. A shoeshiner's life in Luxor. Government at work in Egypt 105
11. A shoeshiner's windfall in Luxor. Russian aid to Egypt 116
12. The Aswan High Dam 136
13. Tragedy in Abu el Feda. Government moves on Education 141

14. Preparing for new arrivals in Abu el Feda. Sadat woos the masses while tension heightens along the Canal 152

15. Winter ends in Luxor. Preparing for war in Cairo . 172

16. New arrivals in Abu el Feda. The extended ceasefire and Israel's reaction to Egypt's proposal for withdrawal from the Canal 178

Epilogue 188

Foreword

David wrote the manuscript for this book in 1971 while we were living in Cairo and he was working for London newspapers *The Sunday Times* and the *Daily Express*. He covered the crisis engendered by the Jordanian civil war, the death of President Nasser and the subsequent rise to power of Anwar el Sadat. He also travelled to Upper Egypt for the opening of the Aswan High Dam, and to Sudan to cover the war in the South. In between these events we went by train to Luxor and rode bicycles around the monuments in the Valley of the Kings. As David explains in his introduction, he was struck by how little the significant political events of the time appeared to concern the local people. Now in hindsight it can be seen that these events were a determined build-up to the 1973 Yom Kippur war with Israel and the subsequent separate peace treaty between Egypt and Israel. On our return to London we typed out his manuscript together on our Olivetti typewriters and after several unsuccessful attempts to interest publishers there the manuscript was left to languish in a drawer.

Meanwhile we returned to Australia and then back to the Middle East in 1977 where we remained for six years, living in Amman, Jordan. This time David was working as foreign correspondent for Australian newspapers *The Age* in Melbourne and *The Sydney Morning Herald*. From Amman he travelled widely around the Arab world and Iran and was a frequent visitor to Israel. He reported on the fall of the Shah of Iran, the Iran/Iraq war from both front lines, the civil war in Lebanon, Middle East peace moves including the 1977 visit to Jerusalem of President Sadat of Egypt, and the subsequent assassination of Sadat. He obtained a rare interview with Ali Khamenei, who later took over as Supreme Leader of Iran following the death of Ayatollah Khomeini, and interviewed other Middle East leaders including Yasser Arafat.

David's novel *A Road from Damascus* first published in paperback in 1992 by The Poppy Press Australia derives from that time and experience. His later novel *The Baghdad Chameleon* published by The Poppy Press Australia in paperback in 2012 derives from subsequent events in the Middle East and his many visits back to the area.

This publication of *Shining the Boot of a Nation* follows the e-book edition published in 2014. I am grateful to our dear friend Celia Walls who re-typed the original typescript into digital format.

Susan Balderstone, July 2015.

Introduction

As a newspaper correspondent in Egypt I had been reporting the events following the death of President Nasser, the transition to a new government and the dominant news story which of course had been the continuing dispute with Israel. Then one day, on February 4, 1971 to be exact, I noted an item in all the major Cairo newspapers reporting that the Permanent Committee on Mothers' Day had decided to celebrate the day on March 21 "and for one week". If not before it struck me then that the majority of Egyptians were not concerned with the events which obsessed me and the world. That is what this book is about.

Map

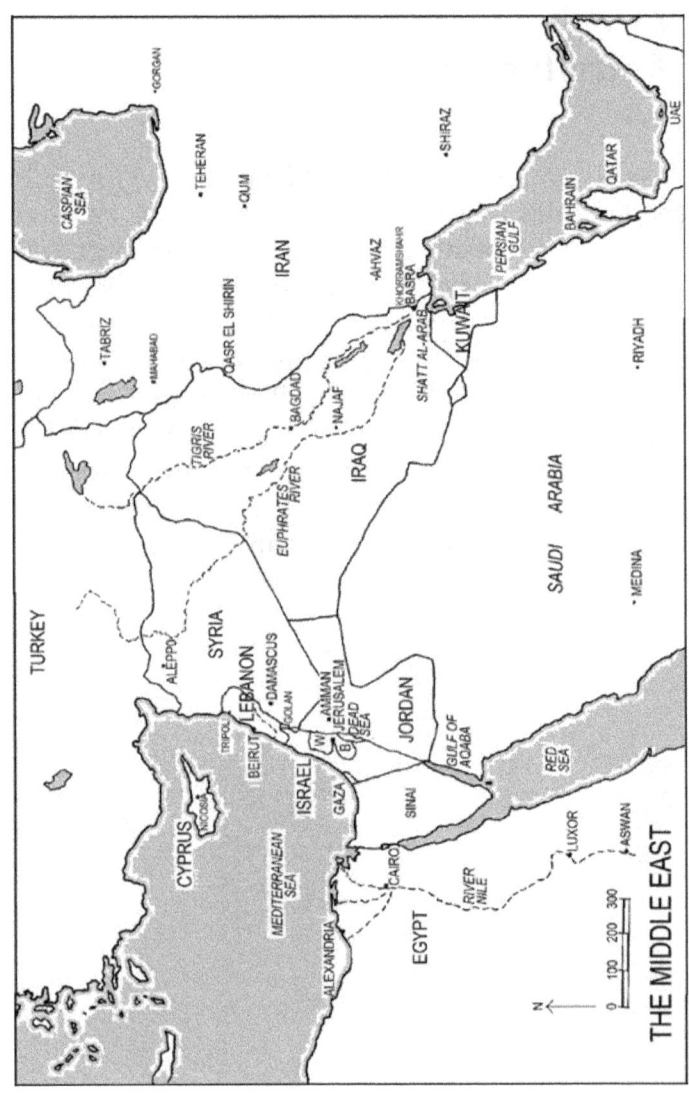

1. A shoeshine in Abu el Feda Street. Sadat addresses the National Assembly

Navigators on the Nile River have always known they can sail south and drift on the tide north. God made the long river that way. It makes life for the felucca man easy for he can sail upstream to pick up his cargo and drift downstream to the cities along the river's banks, including today Cairo. A special river it may be, but in this respect, it does obey the normal worldly rules regarding gravity. And overloaded boats sink just as they do elsewhere.

Hassan broke from his shoeshining to glance across the river. He rather disinterestedly laughed probably for the sake of the client, if client is the word for a person having his shoes shined, and got back to the polishing. Nothing special, nothing funny for Hassan: it was just part of the passing days.

On the river a giant felucca loaded with sand was drifting sideways down the stream. So full was it that water was almost shipping in over the sides. The two men, dressed as all the fellahin dressed in striped galabias, were frantic. One was furiously pumping the handle of a simple mechanism in the middle of the boat and as a result a small trickle of water was being excreted from a hose over the side. The other preferred to enlist the help of his god and was equally enthusiastically prostrating himself on the raised bow section of the boat. After ten minutes or so of praying to the east he jumped up from his straw mat and flung himself towards the centre of the boat to relieve his friend. Probably because there were too many other boats on the Nile in the same predicament at the same time God had not been able to help. The down-to-earth pump was obviously thought to be more effective - at least in the time available.

The river and the overloaded boat flowed onwards like Hassan's life with little apparent change. And if there was a change a bystander would be the last to realise it. Hassan himself didn't see the boring monotony of his life. Shoeshining was a good life and it saved the indignity of begging for a few piasters to sustain life for another day. Although Hassan and other shoeshiners had to resort to this sometimes, when, one might say, business was bad.

The shoes shined, Hassan accepted the five piasters handed him. He stood erect, head almost tilting backwards with his eyes surveying the scene along his long, aquiline nose. He stood on the corniche with his back to the river, his galabia blowing in the breeze. Occasionally his sandaled feet would appear from below the faded green stripes of his galabia. He was about six feet in height and thin. One didn't get overweight as a shoeshiner.

He stood thinking, waiting for some more shoes to shine. No one in sight, but he kept looking. There was competition in the shoeshining business: never knew when another shiner would come along and snatch one of the best customers from under your nose. It all depended on which shoeshiner managed to utter the magic words first: "Shoeshine Mister?" Or an even better trick was to just start shining the damned shoes as the owner was stopped in conversation. However this was risky as there was no obligation to pay and then polish would be wasted. Hassan preferred to ask first.

He stood thinking. God knows what about. For certain not about the shoes he had shined. Why think about those, dirty shoes to be made clean? Not about the day, because days were almost always the same. Not about the conversations he was having with all the other regulars hanging about the big residential apartment blocks on the Cairo island of Zamalek. But more about this than any other thing.

It was a tree-lined street and the sun from the cloudless sky was cutting distinct shadows on the dirt road. It was a residential street, or as residential as streets went in Egypt. There were small shops as well as multi-storied apartment blocks with the daily washing hanging, dripping from the balconies of the flats. A lot of foreigners lived in the flats and certainly only the more well-to-do Egyptians. But all this was good for Hassan: five or even ten piasters instead of two. Also the shoes were usually in better condition so it was better in two ways.

Hassan stood there noting the movements of the people all day. He knew all the cars and who they belonged to and whether the owner was a good try or not. It was a lot of luck, Hassan thought. If only everyone would have their shoes shined every day he would be, well, if not rich, at least well off. But then no point wishing that, nobody ever seemed to have shoes cleaned every day. Just when he had time or had five piasters in his pocket. But if only it was true. He could perhaps then afford a room somewhere with a permanent bed instead of depending upon a friend's kindness. But then that would be a tie also. Always feel obliged to go home for the night, not the sense of freedom. In any case in Egypt it hardly ever rained and the river bank was as good a place as any to sleep. Better, he thought, always running water.

Suddenly Hassan's eyes jumped into focus. He watched a foreigner walk down some steps opposite and make his way along the footpath beside the street. Like some animal after prey, Hassan picked up his box of equipment and crossed the road. Walking faster than the foreigner and in an arc Hassan swept up behind the unsuspecting man.

"Hello friend," said Hassan.

"Hello," I replied.

"English?"

"No, not English," I again replied.

"Not English eh . . .not English eh."

"No."

"Want a shoeshine?"

"No thank you."

"No shoeshine . . .?"

"No."

"What are you carrying those shoes for?" Hassan persisted.

"I am taking them to be mended," I replied.

The conversation, limited as it was continued as we rounded the corner and made our way up a side street to some shops where a shoemaker had his shop.

"Sure no shine?"

"No thank you."

"Mister business very bad today, could you give five piasters and I clean your shoes tomorrow?" pleaded Hassan.

The two stopped dead. "Alright clean my shoes," I said.

Happily he began his task. He had a green shoe cleaner's box with a foot stand on the top. On the sides there were stacked several bottles of liquid cleaners and different colours of polish. "Where did you learn English?"

"I worked fourteen years for an Englishman who drank a bottle of whisky every night," replied Hassan.

"Really?"

"Yes, a whole bottle. Too much eh?"

"Too much."

"Where you from if not English?"

"Australia."

"Austria?"

"No Australia," I emphasised.

"Oh Australia. Very good," said Hassan. "Very good."

The shining continued and the shoes began to look like new. Hassan then turned to the other pair which were on their way to the repairers. "Like them cleaned also?"

"No thank you, I am getting them repaired."

"I will just brush them then."

After insisting it was not necessary, I gave in: "Alright."

"Good."

"How much will that be then?"

"As you like."

"No damn it, not as I like. How much?"

"Fifteen piasters then."

"Fifteen piasters," I said in surprise?

"Yes, fifteen."

"Here is ten."

"Thank you." Hassan pocketed the money and then returned to the first pair of shoes and gave them a final brush. He began chuckling not too subtly under his breath. Then he suddenly exploded in laughter. "You know mister," he said hardly able to hold back his laughter, "You know Mister how much a shoeshine costs in Egypt?"

"No."

"Two piasters only because the people they are very poor," he said with no intention of refunding the change.

"Really," I said trying to be terribly sporting about the whole thing and the honesty of the man. We then parted. But ever afterwards Hassan's greeting would be: "Hello friend".

Hassan made his way back around the corner and to his regular spot on the other side of the road by the river. He resumed his stance and again surveyed the scene through glazed eyes.

The sun was slowly falling from the late summer sky. The great orange ball was throwing a warm light onto the buildings in the street named Abu el Feda, and indeed the street itself. The dusty green leaves on the trees lining the riverside were taking on an orange shade from the setting sun. Hassan looked up into the trees and then along the road. Then into a tree which was directly in line with the sun. He squinted as he looked at the sun through the tree which then just looked like a black silhouette of a tree. The sun and the tree were fused abstract.

It had been not exactly another eventful day, but another day. Eventful enough for Hassan, though. It was not every day that he got a chance to practise his English which, as he realised himself, was surprisingly good for a shoeshiner.

He crossed the road to speak with Dokki, the caretaker-cum-porter of a block of flats. He asked him whether he could possibly leave his shining box with him for the night. Save him carrying it home, or wherever he went as he didn't exactly have a place he could call home. Dokki went through the normal procedure of refusing and then agreeing to allow Hassan's box to be left under the staircase.

"By the Prophet I will clean your shoes tomorrow for no charge," Hassan told Dokki.

"By the Prophet you will too," said Dokki as he waved a farewell to Hassan.

Hassan made his way up the street, galabia flowing in the breeze, ending another day of work. Somewhere to sleep was all that was needed now. And something to eat, he thought. He continued his way through Cairo's streets oblivious, like at least three quarters of his countrymen, of the events that evening at the country's National Assembly. Sure he knew Nasser was dead, almost everyone did, but not what was happening now.

***

Anwar el Sadat made his way across the platform of the National Assembly. He walked as if slow marching with very deliberate steps to the dais from which he would deliver his nomination speech. He had already received what was officially described as the unanimous support of members of the National Assembly. All he needed now was the approval of the country at a referendum and then he would be President of Egypt - Nasser's successor.

On reaching the dais the extremely trim man in tailored suit paused and acknowledged the standing ovation from the members of the National Assembly, Egypt's parliament which provided a forum for discussion rather than a legislative body. It mainly rubber-stamped all legislature put before it by the president or the cabinet. The members, this night dressed some in conventional suits and others in formal galabias, by procedure had to belong to Egypt's Arab Socialist Union, the country's only legal political body or party. The National Assembly building was circular and domed and press men were seated in a gallery around the walls. On the floor to the right of the platform, press and television cameramen had set up their equipment. Even before the revolution in July 1952 the building had housed the National Assembly.

The applause subsided and Sadat began to speak. He pledged to follow the path of the late President Nasser and to carry on his work. He noted that the struggle for the liberation of all the Arab territories occupied in the Six Day War of 1967 had to be pursued and the rights of the people of Palestine had to be maintained in full.

"We are called upon to continue the struggle for the unity of the Arab nation and to fight the enemies of our nation, namely Israel, international Zionism and world imperialism," he said. He made special mention of the "special friendship" binding the United Arab Republic and the Soviet Union. He pointed to the policy of Nasser which had been to befriend those who were friendly towards Egypt and to be hostile to those who stood against her.

In this nomination speech Anwar el Sadat gave the first official indication that the new government would be collective. He made it clear that he would not take on all the tasks that Nasser had shouldered. "It is not in my capacity, nor in the capacity of any one person to shoulder all the burdens the late President assumed. Consequently re-allocation of responsibilities is necessary in order to guarantee the proper discharge of the trust placed in the hands of the government."

Between the time of this speech on October 8 and the national referendum on October 15, there was much speculation as to what form this collective government would take. But naturally enough no official word was disclosed until following the nation's approval of Sadat.

The referendum was billed as a democratic and secret ballot. It was a "yes" or "no" vote as Sadat was the only candidate nominated by the National Assembly. To get the Assembly's nomination Sadat had had to get the support of two thirds of the members. Had he failed to get this percentage another vote would have been taken at which he would have had to achieve an absolute majority. Watching the voting in the National Assembly, as I did, it was quite obvious that some of the members did not place a card in the ballot box. However a unanimous vote of support was announced. The members who did not cast a vote were most probably not dissenting but merely knew the procedure well enough to know that their vote would not alter the result. They were obviously correct.

Prior to the actual people's referendum, *Al Ahram*, Egypt's most influential newspaper and edited by Mohammed Heikal, then the minister for National Guidance, told its readers that the important thing was to vote, not whether the opinion was 'yes' or 'no'. Nevertheless, and not surprisingly, it supported Sadat.

In villages, cities and towns throughout Egypt the secret ballot took place. A friend who took a look at a polling station in Cairo had the following conversation with a woman official outside the station, a school I believe:

"How is it going?" said he.

"Oh very well, everyone has voted 'yes' so far."

"But I thought it was secret?" he questioned.

"Yes, it is but we know that everyone has voted 'yes'."

Secret or not, a ninety percent 'yes' vote was recorded. This incredibly high percentage was gained not by any wilful rigging on the part of the government, but rather by over enthusiasm on the part of the local officials, the system which tosses up only one candidate, and of course the genuine support for the man himself, especially as to the people, he had received the unanimous support of their representatives in the National Assembly.

2. Events surrounding the death of President Nasser

The memory of Nasser was still strong when the people went to the polls on October 15, 1970 to approve Anwar el Sadat. It was only two weeks since he had died shortly after he farewelled the last of the Arab leaders following the satisfactory conclusion of the Arab summit convened over the crisis in Jordan.

In Jordan fierce fighting had been taking place between King Hussein's army and the Palestinian resistance guerrillas. Although the exact number of dead was not known, it reached several thousand. The crisis was mainly responsible, together with later skirmishes, for considerably weakening the resistance. As well as weakening the resistance it considerably weakened Arab unity although at the conclusion of the summit held at the Nile Hilton Hotel in Cairo, King Hussein and Yasser Arafat, chairman of the Palestinian Resistance Central Committee, cheerily shook hands more as if concluding a bowls match than a bloody battle.

Hailed as an Arab Summit convened to find a solution to the Jordanian crisis, it became even before the heads of state had time to shake their greetings, merely a gathering and not a summit. While the late arrivals were motorcading the guarded way from Cairo airport to the Nile Hilton, Egypt's National Guidance Minister, Mohammed Heikal, was telling correspondents that it was not a summit in the proper sense of the word. It lacked the "pomp and ceremonies" which surrounded such affairs. He preferred the term "gathering".

Confusion was not restricted to the question of what to label the meeting. This centred partly on Nasser's relationship with King Hussein. On the debit side Nasser could never forgive Hussein for his harsh attitude towards the Palestinians and his not unfriendly relationship with Israel. But on the credit side he knew that it was essential to have Hussein's support for any peace to be achieved out of the United States-initiated peace plan. Nasser, so intent on getting peace, may have tolerated a quick blow by Hussein to quell the tide of Palestinian guerrilla activities within Jordan.

From the start of the summit it was clear that Hussein would not get much support. In fact until King Feisal's late arrival it was hard to find one delegate who would speak up for Hussein. Kuwait was the possible exception and her support would have been mainly due to her necessity to keep the support of King Feisal.

Although not entirely unexpected, the first drama of the summit came on the first night. After a day of discussions about Syria's intervention in the crisis, Dr Atassy, then the Syrian leader, finding himself without support, announced he was leaving. He finally left the following morning accompanied by Major Al-Khuwaildy al-Hamida, a member of the Libyan Revolution Command Council who was sent, it seemed, by the leaders left in Cairo with the brief of a watchdog.

With the desert sand around the airport still in the air following the departure of Atassy's jet, the delegation, dispatched by the summit the previous day under the leadership of Sudan's President Gaafar Nimeiry, arrived back with a ceasefire agreement between Hussein and two of four Palestinian leaders released by Hussein after a request by the delegation. But before they even reached the Hilton, reports were arriving of fresh fighting. And a cable later that evening from Yasser Arafat to Nasser killed any remaining hope Nimeiry may have held regarding the success of his mission. Arafat told Nasser the ceasefire agreement had taken the Palestinians by surprise and had been concluded without the knowledge of the resistance. He said the colleagues who had agreed to it were not in a position that allowed them to speak for the revolution.

The following day Nimeiry headed a fresh mission to Amman this time intent on meeting Arafat, a meeting which in fact took place.

The failure of the ceasefire agreement arranged on Nimeiry's first mission was probably also due to dissention within the ranks of the Jordanian Army.

Arafat's cable to Nasser obviously brought to light embarrassment the Arab leaders felt over the first agreement. At the following press briefing the spokesman for the leaders said at length that the Palestinian guerrillas had proved their right to exist.

The summit from the start was a balancing act with Hussein on one side and Arafat on the other. Towards the end of the week the Arab leaders were improving their technique and what had looked hopeless was becoming quite a polished trick. The main outcome of this summit was a declaration which has subsequently been labelled the Cairo Accord. It aimed at achieving peace between the resistance and the army and set up a peace-keeping committee under the direction of Bahi Ladgham, then the Tunisian premier. For some time peace was maintained but inevitably after a couple of months fighting began to occur again.

Shortly after President Gamal Abdul Nasser, the host of the summit, had performed the last of his official duties, he was dead. The death was caused by a sudden heart attack while he was at Cairo Airport seeing off the ruler of Kuwait, who was the last of the Arab kings and heads of state to leave Cairo. He evidently felt a pang of pain in his chest while standing beside the aircraft of the Kuwaiti ruler. He asked that his car be bought over to where he was standing. He was immediately taken to his home where doctors attended him. But they could not save his life.

Several government ministers had gathered at Nasser's home as the news spread. Vice President Sadat chaired a meeting and it was decided to declare a state of top emergency among the armed forces. It was also decided to remove the body to the Kubbeh Republican Palace, the official quarters of the head of state. Sadat was also given the task of informing the nation over the radio and television. Ironically, eighteen years earlier he had been the revolutionary Free Officer selected to tell the nation that the revolution had taken place. He was also made interim president.

I was standing in the main Cairo radio and television building when Sadat announced Nasser's death. Suddenly terrible screams filled the building. With tears in their eyes men and women began leaving the building, supporting each other in their grief. Men were literally hitting their heads against brick walls. It was a tragic hour.

In the street outside the building men, women and children were gathering, chanting and demonstrating their grief. As if attracted to the place from which the dreadful news had emanated, they paraded up and down. Throughout Cairo this continued for three days until after the days of initial mourning and the funeral were over. The official mourning did last for forty days, however. The news came about eleven o'clock in the evening and within an hour the city of four and a half million people was thronged with people. Traffic in some areas was at a standstill as people swarmed along the roads chanting what seemed to be a mixture of prayer and protest. People came from everywhere that night to be with their countrymen. They gathered in thousands around the Kubbeh Republican Palace where the body had been taken.

As the days before the funeral passed Egyptians came from the extremities of the country to Cairo for the ceremony. In the evening these people who had ridden into the city on top of trains, in carts, cars or on donkeys and camels, bedded down wherever there was a space. Driving became unusually hazardous as bodies were strewn across the roads in some places.

The daytime hours were also unusual. The men who normally smoked their bubble pipes in street-side cafes had disappeared and many of the cafes were closed. In many respects it was like a deserted city, except in reality there were more people than ever in it. All along the corniche beside the Nile people gathered, especially in front of the Nile Hilton and Shepheard's Hotel where foreign dignitaries were being accommodated.

What exactly the people thought about, it's hard to guess. Peasants were mourning their departed leader, but they were also following their fellow countrymen and it was in some respects as if each person was trying to prove that he or she was more grief-stricken than anyone else.

Nasser's death illustrated explicitly the Muslim-Arab way of death, or perhaps more correctly grief. Whereas most people of European descent placed the emphasis in time of grief on suppressing their emotions, the Egyptians and the Arabs as a whole did not. Hence three days of street demonstrating and chanting in Cairo, and elsewhere in Egypt following the death of the hero president. The details into which *Al Ahram* went in describing the death itself and the events immediately afterwards underline the emphasis placed on the display of grief. On Tuesday September 29, the day after Nasser died, *Al Ahram* reported:

"All those who were present left the room to the family of the great hero to bid him a final farewell. Everything seemed like an appalling nightmare, gripping the whole world and mankind. Those who left the bedroom moved to the study room next door. There they could hear the sobs of the last farewell between the family and its great man. They themselves were in tears, unable to control themselves."

Then later on in the story the scene was described when the ministers met in Nasser's house under the then Vice President Anwar Sadat. "Dr Aziz Sidky (now Minister for Industry) burst out crying, while Sayed Marei left the room not wanting to cry inside the room. Dr Mahmoud Fawzi (now Prime Minister) went on crying in serene sadness."

The funeral was held two days later on Thursday October 1. The most notable exception amongst world statesmen attending was American President Richard Nixon. He instead sent an envoy. Nixon said at the time that he thought it would have been inappropriate for him to have attended the funeral as the United States and Egypt did not have formal diplomatic relations. Sadat, as the new president of Egypt, when questioned some months later by a newsman said he was sorry Nixon had not made the trip to Cairo. He felt it would have done a lot for American-Egyptian relations. Undoubtedly it would have. But it may also have proved embarrassing for Mr Kosygin, the Soviet premier. In spite of the mighty assistance given by the Soviet Union to Egypt, the Egyptians generally were more impressed with the American way of life than the Russian. As an extension of this, Nixon was more of a name than Kosygin, Breznev, or Podgorny.

Amongst the millions of Egyptians in Cairo for the funeral and lining the route of the cortege was a man who could have perhaps been expected not to attend: General Mohammed Neguib. Neguib was thrown up by the revolutionary Free Officers as the first post-1952 revolution leader of Egypt. Neguib played no real part in the revolution itself which was engineered by Nasser, but was given the post of chief executive because the revolutionaries felt someone of standing was needed. However in February 1954 the dissatisfaction of the revolutionaries with Neguib's rule prompted Nasser to take over.

Following the funeral, as if everyone had been so exhausted by the three days of mourning, Cairo returned fairly much to normal. But the many portraits of Nasser remained daubed on the windows of taxis and on billboards for months.

3. Leadership manoeuvrings and the influence of Mohammed Heikal. Life in Abu el Feda

As soon as the news of the death of President Nasser was known speculation had begun as to who his successor might be. Across the Suez Canal in Israel, the news was greeted with some concern. The general feeling there being: the devil you know is better than the devil you don't.

In Egypt the speculation got off to a good start the day following the death when *Al Ahram* printed prominently an obituary to the late leader by Zakaria Mohieddin. Mohieddin had been the man selected by Nasser following the June 1967 defeat by Israel, to succeed him. However then prompted by the call of the people Nasser withdrew his resignation and after only a couple of days took over from Mohieddin. What made the publishing of this obituary so interesting was the fact that the editor of *Al Ahram* was Nasser's long-time confidant and friend Mohammed Heikal, who then held the portfolio of Minister for National Guidance, or Information as it was later called. It was believed that Mohieddin was being thrown up by Heikal as Nasser's successor. Too much could be read into this because Mohieddin had been out of favour with Nasser and had been living out of the public eye. Reports that he was under house arrest seemed to be exaggerated as although police guarded his house this was not an unusual situation in Egypt for any political figure. However it probably would be true enough to say that the

Egyptian Intelligence usually knew his whereabouts - this being rather a tribute to the Intelligence's efficiency than to Mohieddin's importance.

It was later reported from Beirut by Associated Press that Heikal had nominated Mohieddin for the presidential position at a cabinet meeting. This was however publicly denied. This rather dubious story was raised again some weeks later following the referendum by the people supporting Sadat as president. It was announced that Heikal had resigned from his position as Minister for National Guidance. It was thought that Heikal had in fact been ousted for supporting Mohieddin's nomination. But there seemed no real reason to doubt Heikal's own explanation for his resignation as outlined in his weekly column "Frankly Speaking" in *Al Ahram*. Heikal said he was primarily a journalist and wanted to get back to his profession. Although he had been able to continue editing *Al Ahram* during the months he had been minister, he had not been able to devote the time needed for such a job. He also pointed out that he had been in fact drafted by Nasser to do the job and had been extremely reluctant. He explained the whole story:

"But April 26 1970 came and I was surprised to hear of my appointment in the National Guidance portfolio on the radio. Only hours before I had been talking to him (Nasser) and we shifted from one topic to another but the question of portfolio never came up either directly or by intimation. I then took my leave to spend a day outside Cairo and he agreed. Then all of a sudden I heard the news on the radio."

Heikal then hurried back to Cairo and wrote a letter to Nasser asking him to reconsider his decision. Later that same evening Nasser called Heikal to go to his residence to discuss the matter. At the meeting, according to Heikal, Nasser understood the objections, but said that the appointment was final. Heikal accepted the situation on the strength of Nasser's promise that the assignment would be for a minimum of six months and a maximum of twelve.

Heikal decided to resign following the death of Nasser and actually tendered his resignation to interim president Sadat before the referendum. However Sadat requested Heikal to stay on as Minister for National Guidance until after the referendum. Heikal's resignation as explained in the letter to Sadat dated October 3 was based mainly on the fact that he had been drafted by Nasser personally and against his stated wishes, that he wished to return fully to journalism, and that he wished to write his memoirs of Nasser. He said to Sadat: "I sincerely wish that you will not interpret my request as my giving up at a critical time. You know that such a thought has never occurred to me; for you are the man whom he in person has chosen to be his deputy, and at a time he was exposed to the dangers of plots which were being hatched by those whose control and ambitions he had been challenging all his life."

In spite of other wild rumours, Sadat was really the only strong contender for the presidency. As Heikal had said, Sadat had a great claim for the presidency having been chosen by Nasser to be his vice president. Although Nasser's relationship with Sadat had not always been so convivial.

Heikal was undoubtedly the man closest to Nasser and his weekly column in *Al Ahram* was a good indication of Nasser's thinking and the line the government would take on certain issues. It was and continued to be, but to a lesser extent, compulsory reading for any observer of

Egyptian affairs. The friendship undoubtedly gave Heikal great power and advantages as a journalist and he was able to be critical when other journalists would not have dared. He was also able to build the newspaper into a substantial empire by any standards and incorporated side businesses, such as job printing, into the original firm. He was dynamic if not un-assuming and clearly the newspaper became what it was due to him and Nasser's support of him. He appointed extremely worldly executives to support him and walking into the plush Cairo offices was just like walking into any large and successful Western publishing company premises.

It was his very friendship which threw up doubts about his future following the death of Nasser. But he managed to retain a close relationship with successor Sadat, even if things were not as before. The column "Frankly Speaking" ceased to be such a good guide for observers. Heikal did however, on many occasions, prove his friendship with Sadat by arranging interviews for visiting journalists with the new president. Still journalists wishing to interview Sadat went through Heikal and not the Ministry of Information.

Another cause for speculation was the extent of influence exerted by Russia on the appointment of a new leader. It was assumed by many that Russia was taking a considerable interest in the man who was to replace Nasser.

The support Russia had given Egypt militarily, socially and economically fostered the belief that she would play a part in the internal politics. Most of the people who were keen on this theory were predicting other people for the presidency, and still others than the ones finally selected, for the other chief positions. In the event the appointment of Sadat and subsequently Dr Mahmoud Fawzi as Prime Minister seemed a likely Egyptian choice. But granted, the Russians most probably approved.

Speculation about Russian influence tended to be a wholly external game - few Egyptians being interested to play. The masses would go their merry way, Russian influence or no Russian influence, like they would British influence or no British influence.

***

Dokki tossed a dark brown scarf around his head. Then he took up his daily position in Abu el Feda. He looked across the road to the mist settled on top of the river. The road was coated with a film of moisture. Morning and all was quiet. Dokki's job was to look after the block of flats, acting as a porter, caretaker and messenger. Not a bad living and it was not hard work. Every month the people in each flat would give him an Egyptian pound. So there were thirty pounds for a start. In a land where it was said you could live on five piasters a day that was not bad. And he got his accommodation free. Two rooms, half a garage and another boarded up section giving him another room for the television. Yes television: Dokki was the envy of all his friends.

Dokki, a Muslim, had four children: two boys and two girls. Compared with most people in Egypt he was well off. Sabra, his eldest child, helped around the building. He sold beer and other bottled drinks to the residents at a piaster profit, and she helped him with that. Sabra also helped by cleaning the floors and minding her baby brother. She was eight but did not go to school. Although it was compulsory a lot of children did not go. Waste of time when you can make yourself useful doing business.

Dokki sat on the chair beside the road, his daily position. From there he watched the passing parade and saw what there was to see. He thought about the television he had watched the night before. But that was not all. He was engrossed in thought this morning when Hassan ambled along the street to take up his shoeshining position, across the street. Hassan walked up to Dokki to collect the box of polishes and brushes he had left overnight.

"Sa'id Dokki," Hassan said in greeting.

Silence.

"Sa'id Dokki," Hassan repeated.

Still silence. So Hassan reached under the stairs to collect the tools of his trade. He again repeated his greeting to Dokki and this time he got some response.

"Naharak sa'id," Dokki replied.

"By the Prophet, you were deep in thought," said Hassan.

"Yes," said Dokki. He had some news. His wife was pregnant again. Another child was on the way.

"Pregnant?"

"Pregnant," said Dokki.

"Another baby, that is good."

"Yes that is good," Dokki said half-heartedly.

"Not good?" questioned Hassan sensing something.

"Yes good, but not good."

Then he explained to Hassan how four children were really enough and that the cost of looking after another child would make a difference. Hassan shook his head in acknowledgement of the argument being put before him. But then, thought Hassan, plenty of people had more than four children? And they were a lot worse off than Dokki.

"By the Prophet you promised me a shine," demanded Dokki, changing the subject.

"Me?"

"Yes, by the Prophet, you."

"No, not today."

"Yes."

After the daily exchange, Hassan got down to the task of cleaning Dokki's shoes. "No point cleaning them when the ground is damp, but if you want them done I'll do them."

The day continued. The hours passed. Hassan had moved across the road and was sitting on the wall overlooking the river. Today he was not standing, but his eyes kept a keen lookout for customers. The day passed like all days did with little event. But it was rather pleasant sitting with the sun on your back and the light breeze in the air: not too windy or dusty, just pleasant.

"Hello Mister," said Dokki to me as I passed. The only English he knew.

"Hello my friend," came the voice from across the road. "Like a shine today?"

"No."

"No shine, just a brush then?"

I gave in and we started talking. About nothing in particular. Then Dokki crossed the road and approached beaming.

"This man doesn't speak English, my friend," said Hassan seeing Dokki approach. "No English," he repeated proudly displaying his best English.

"Really."

"Yes, no English."

I nodded to Dokki and we struck up a conversation through the interpreter-cum-shoeshiner Hassan.

"How are you?" I said timidly, starting on a simple topic.

And what a performance. Hassan lifted his head with a painfully bored expression on his face and uttered "Izzaiyak." Then he returned to the shoes to await the next scintillating piece of conversation.

Dokki answered: "Kwaiyis."

Hassan lifted his head from the shoes again and mouthed "He feels good."

Then it was Dokki's turn to ask a question. In fact it was more of a statement than a question. "Are you an Australian?" he asked, fully knowing that I was.

I answered the question when it came to me through Hassan: "Yes."

Hassan told Dokki I said "yes". And Dokki fired another question: "There is another Australian living in the same flats as you. Did you know? "

"Really," I replied. "Which flat?" Hassan quickly relayed my answer.

The full answer cannot have been relayed though for the next statement from Dokki was: "He is very rich. And he speaks Arabic."

Then suddenly Hassan cut us short and nodded his head in the direction of the entrance stairs to the flats opposite. "There he is". The three of us dubiously watched the man descend the stairs and hail a cab. When he had found a cab Hassan said: "That was him."

Then we talked about his English. And the story about the Englishman with whom he had worked for fourteen years came out again. Presumably he wasn't cleaning shoes for the Englishman for fourteen years. But it never was mentioned what Hassan did. Probably wasn't important to him. The main thing was the money for the food for the stomach for the life every day.

Another pair of shoes walked up and Hassan rapidly lost interest in his English and my shoes. Quickly he put a final polish on them and I was finished.

"There ten piasters," said Hassan.

I handed him five.

"Not good shine?" he questioned.

"Yes good shine, but only five today."

"Goodbye friend," he said turning to the new pair of shoes which were by now resting on his box. And Dokki joined the conversation. The man spoke Arabic.

It was Dokki's turn to outdo Hassan. He talked with the man about the television they had both watched the night before. Hassan, having no television, not even a radio, continued the shine. If only everyone would get every pair of their shoes cleaned every day then perhaps he could not only have his own room and bed but also a television. But then no-one even gets one pair of shoes cleaned every day let alone every pair. Wishful thinking.

Up the street rode a man on a tricycle. Not a child's toy, but a tricycle the same size as a full-sized bicycle. And still more unlike a child's tricycle was the fact that the two wheels were at the front and the single wheel at the back - it was in reverse. On the two front wheels was supported a tray affair. It was in fact a small man-driven truck. It was painted blue seemingly to match the man who was riding it. Or perhaps the man was dressed in a blue boiler suit to match the tricycle he was propelling. The tricycle was loaded with six portable gas containers all painted the same shade of blue. The man was pedalling very slowly and deliberately obviously because of the weight of the load. But this slow motion took on a slightly surrealistic look in the morning sun.

"Sa'id, Dokki," called the rather puffed man from his tricycle.

"Sa'id," came the acknowledgement.

"Sa'id, Hassan."

"Sa'id, Mahmoud," said Hassan quickly adding: "Like a shine?" But the sales pitch was ignored.

Dokki moved across the road and approached Mahmoud on his tricycle. After a short conversation Mahmoud unloaded one of his gas cylinders heaved it on to his shoulders, and made his way into Dokki's block of flats.

"It's for number fifteen," called Dokki behind him.

Mahmoud staggered up the steps, across the foyer and into the lift. Dokki crossed the road and took up his position beside Hassan. The two just stood. They did not talk. Nothing to talk about when nothing special ever happens. Hassan stood erect again with his head tilted backwards slightly. The two were a contrast. Hassan in his peasant's galabia and Dokki in a more formal, but similar outfit. But Dokki wore a turban affair around his head. And on top of this a brown scarf was wrapped. God knows why, for it was still late summer and the sun was still giving the days considerable heat. Hassan did not have anything on his head and only sandals on his feet. But they did not show much except when the wind blew his ground-length galabia from his feet. The wind also disclosed Hassan's spindly body. It blew the outfit around him disclosing his form.

They just stood. No-one needed their shoes shined. Or, Hassan thought, plenty of people needed their shoes shined. They stood, and the stillness of the passing hours was only disturbed by the tooting of cars' horns and Hassan occasionally saying: "Shine Mister?"

Strangely, in spite of the tooting of horns and the general bustle along the street of vendors selling every conceivable thing, beggars asking for piasters, young people walking hand in hand, Dokki's and Hassan's day was quite serene. They looked like observers standing across the road. They had been there all day. They had been first to arrive. They had seen everything happen. They were observers, but they were part of the scene as well. All that was happening they saw. Everything which was happening they had seen before. Everything that was happening they would see again. God willing.

Mahmoud came out of the building again and Dokki broke off observing and crossed the road to make sure all had gone alright. Mahmoud was carrying the empty container having deposited the full one. He literally threw the empty container into the tray on his tricycle, hopped on to the seat behind, and put his feet on the pedals. But he didn't ride off. He talked to Dokki. He passed the time of day. Dokki told him he was to have another child.

"By the Prophet that is good."

"Yes it is good."

"It is not good?" questioned Mahmoud having also sensed a feeling of doubt in Dokki's voice.

"Yes, it is good, but it is not good."

Dokki said that the social service worker had told him and his wife not to have any more children. Because four was enough. But anyway she was pregnant. And she was happy about it having never been too keen on the idea of contraception. It wasn't natural. And against the teachings of the Prophet Mohammed, or was it?

"I see," said Mahmoud with understanding. "But five is not much more than four. One more will surely not make that much difference."

A smile came over Dokki's face. "No I suppose it isn't: five instead of four, only one more mouth to feed."

Mahmoud stood high, putting all his weight on one pedal. The tricycle began slowly to move. Without saying goodbye Dokki withdrew to his seat in front of the flats and thought over what Mahmoud had said. Mahmoud slowly picked up momentum and headed off down the street, waving to Hassan as he went, and then rounded the corner which led to the gas shop where he would pick up another batch of containers for delivery.

No parting greeting had been necessary between Dokki and Mahmoud. They would see each other many times again before the sun set. Anyway there was always tomorrow.

Nothing had yet been built next to Dokki's block of flats. Dokki had made use of this. He had his own irrigation scheme and was producing vegetables of many kinds. But as well he had a goat tethered by a eucalyptus tree. A sign of affluence it was really. It provided more than enough milk for his family. Goat's milk is good for children, he had been told. Anything straight from the animal that you don't have to buy from the shop is good, thought Dokki.

Dokki was in fact the envy of all his friends around. He was really well off compared with most of them. He didn't have to clean shoes, or beg, or even depend on the kindness of some person or other. He was self-supporting. Dokki himself was proud of this. For life he had this job caretaking this building and for life he had a home. He had bought the goat when it was just a few days old for a pound. The owner thought it was going to die and sold it cheaply. Not that a young goat was worth much in Egypt. The feeding was the bug-bear. But there was plenty of green grass along the river bank so that was no problem.

Dokki was in fact in a class above most of his friends. He knew it also. But he talked with the others because everyone is different from everyone else. After all the shoeshiner Hassan was better off than the beggar asking for baksheesh. He was better off than the women in black carrying their new born babies around asking for money. They were a sorry sight. Occasionally some rich man out of the flats would drop them a piaster or two, thinking this was easier than the constant theatrical weeping for the small one in the arms of the beggar. They usually went in twos these women. God knows why. Probably so there was someone to talk to when no hand-out was imminent.

Hassan kept his vigilant watch for clients. A bad day it was: only two or three pairs of shoes done all day: not good enough to sustain life. And what is more two had been the shoes of his poor friends who paid only two piasters. Hardly worth getting down to put the spit and polish on the leather. But he had. A principle of a shoeshiner is never reject a shoe. Better a piaster than no piaster. He was almost asleep standing up. The warm sun soothed his back which was cricked from sleeping on the hard ground the night before.

Dokki began to doze off as well. The day was like that. Like most days in Cairo it made you want to just fall off to sleep. In fact when afternoon came everyone did go to sleep, the shops closed, everyone went home and slept. But it was still morning so Dokki was trying to keep his eyes open.

He was dark-skinned compared with Mahmoud or Hassan. He was from Upper Egypt originally but had moved to Cairo to make use of the opportunities the big city gave. No television for one thing where he came from. Goats, yes, but not thirty pounds a month.

The day passed, Dokki sitting on his chair, Hassan cleaning the occasional pair of shoes.

4. The Free Officers and the 1952 revolution

Mohammed Heikal had made the point in his letter of resignation to Anwar el Sadat. Sadat clearly had a great claim to the presidency having been Nasser's choice for vice president. The two had been friends since long before the revolution of July 26, 1952. But Sadat had at times been out of favour. He had been vice president of Egypt twice, the job having been taken away from him once following the Six Day War. He had resumed office the December before Nasser died, that was December 1969. It was quite conceivable that had Nasser lived, Sadat would have slipped again from favour as he had before. But as events have shown, things did not happen that way.

Nasser and Sadat shared an undeniable concern for their country. They were sincere and idealistic young men together. They lived with the same dream for the same country. They were young Army officers together and spent many hours talking around camp fires after days on manoeuvres, with other young officers. They were together when the revolution was conceived, but had to wait a long time for it to be hatched. They both abhorred the continual occupation of Egypt from outside by Britain and others. They equally hated the monarchy and the government which was supported by it. They wanted an Egypt for Egyptians.

Before the revolution, as always, Nasser was the tactician. It was his yes or no that decided the next move.

It was he who gave the go ahead or vetoed any plans. Sadat appreciated his sound sense. Sadat gave many examples of this in his book *Revolt on the Nile*, which tells the story of the 1952 revolution. One case was in February 1945 when Nokrachy Pasha became prime minister of Egypt following the assassination of Ahmed Maher. Nokrachy Pasha visited the then British Ambassador, Lord Killearn (formerly Sir Miles Lampson) to emphasise Egypt's national interests. Lord Killearn did not receive the Egyptian prime minister but merely exchanged a few words at the foot of the staircase and lost patience as soon as Nokrachy Pasha began to speak of Egypt's national interests. This, says Sadat, caused widespread public indignation when it became known.

"I went to see Gamal Abdul Nasser and put up a plan for revenge. My idea was to blow up the British Embassy and everybody in it. The Popular Section (of the Revolutionary Committee) would carry out the operation. Gamal listened attentively and then shook his head and said no. He reminded me of the terrible reprisals which had followed the murder in 1924 of Sir Lee Stack, Sirdar and Governor General of the Sudan. 'The tragedy must not be repeated,' said Abdul Nasser."

After years of waiting for the revolution, when Nasser actually gave the word, Sadat himself nearly missed the event as he was taking his children to the cinema. "I decided to give my children a treat and I took them to an open air cinema near my home. In the meantime, Gamal, who was summoning the conspirators himself, called for me in his famous little Austin car. He called again an hour later and finding me still out, left a note, which said quite simply: 'It happens tonight. Rendezvous at Abdul Hakim's, eleven p.m.' My heart leaped. I left my astonished and anxious children with the porter and bounded up the stairs. I tore off my civilian clothes and hurriedly threw on my uniform. In five minutes I was at the wheel of my car. But the place of rendezvous when I got there was deserted. The operation had already begun."

But Sadat caught up with things and was the man who eventually announced the coup to the nation over the radio.

President Sadat wrote another book which was in fact about Nasser and was entitled: *This is Your Uncle Gamal, My Son*.

Born in 1918, in Meit Abou el Kom, Markaz Tala, Menufieh, Sadat attended military academy and graduated in 1938. Following graduation he was posted to the signals corps where he stayed until 1942. In 1942, he was tried by a court made up of two British judges and an Egyptian judge on a charge of conspiring against the security of the state in time of war. It was as a result of his association with two German spies in Cairo. He was sentenced to imprisonment in a detention camp at Miniah on October 8. He escaped from the same camp two years later in November 1944. He was again imprisoned in 1946 for two years and this kept him out of the 1948 Palestine War - much to his annoyance and frustration.

Imprisonment naturally enough gave him no real love for the British, although by 1971 it would be hard to say that he was anti-British and his government had in fact taken many steps towards improving its relationship with the once-occupying power.

Sadat was one of the eleven original Free Officers led by Nasser who staged the revolution, and ever afterwards he was rewarded for his loyalty. He was immediately appointed a Minister of State holding several portfolios.

Subsequently he was a member of the Revolution Tribunal, Secretary General of the National Union and Chairman of the Islamic Conference and Speaker of the country's National Assembly from 1960 until 1968.

He was appointed vice president the first time and made a member of the presidential council in February 1964. However the position of vice president was abandoned in 1968. He was then elected a member of the Arab Socialist Union's Supreme Executive Committee and Secretary of the A.S.U.'s political affairs committee. However on December 20, 1969 Anwar el Sadat was again appointed vice president by decree of President Nasser. On this occasion Sadat was summoned by Nasser early in the morning. Not until Sadat arrived was he informed that he was to be appointed vice president. Nasser immediately carried out the appointment.

So Anwar el Sadat had a claim, but of course Zakaria Mohieddin also had a claim using this logic. Sadat, true, had been Nasser's choice for vice president, but Mohieddin had been appointed Nasser's successor by Nasser himself, in 1967. And this was at a time when Sadat was vice president.

There was no reason, however, to believe that Sadat had any ambitions for the presidency. He probably never had any notions of the kind because of his similar age to Nasser and Nasser's lifelong occupation of the position. However he should have known, more than his fellow countrymen, of Nasser's heart complaints. Nasser's illnesses had begun as long ago as 1958 when doctors discovered he was a diabetic. His health slowly, but not drastically, deteriorated until 1968, when he was scheduled to visit Moscow. His doctors advised him to be examined by Soviet physicians. But on his way to

Moscow he was struck with pain and once in Moscow went into the Berbeikha Hospital for a complete check-up. During the check-up it was discovered that it was a case of diabetes complications. Early in 1969 the pains disappeared greatly due to treatment, but in September, whilst in Russia it was found that he had a blood clot in the front artery of his heart. His condition slowly deteriorated due to the pressure of work, and lack of adequate rest and relaxation.

Only a week before he died his doctors had ordered him to relax. It was in the midst of the Jordanian crisis and he merely pointed out to the doctors that every minute scores of men and women were dying in Jordan. "Don't you see, it's a race against death," was his indignant, and as it turned out, ironical statement.

5. Sadat forms a government

As early as his nomination speech Sadat had indicated that he would not take over all the tasks Nasser had assumed. It was to be a collective government. This was an incredibly sane move on the part of Sadat as he was correct, no man could shoulder all the tasks Nasser had shouldered. In the event it turned out that his prime minister, Dr Mahmoud Fawzi, generally speaking operated the government machinery and Sadat was left, or so it seemed, to attend to the war.

His appointment of four deputy premiers each in charge of a sector of the government, gave him a compact inner cabinet for high-level and quick decision making. It was a decision which enabled Egypt to be properly brought back to cabinet government. Previously cabinet meetings were long and unwieldy. The four deputy premiers were Dr Aziz Sidki, Minister for Industry, Sayed Marei, Minister of Agriculture, Mahmoud Riad, Minister for Foreign Affairs, and Sharawi Gomaa, Minister for the Interior. The cabinet in other respects was very similar to the last Nasser cabinet.

In a country at war it was inevitable that the foreign affairs side of the government became the most well known. Indeed on the international scene the three names that were attached most closely to the name of Egypt were Sadat, Fawzi and Riad, the foreign minister. However it would be wrong to forget the power of other members of the cabinet, particularly the other deputy premiers. In particular Sharawi Gomaa, the interior minister, controlled

Egypt's major intelligence service, which in a country like Egypt, was a great source of political power.

Gomaa was in fact the cause himself for much speculation following the appointment of Sadat, but before the cabinet and the premiership of Dr Fawzi was announced. It was thought at that stage that a ruling triumvirate of Sadat, Gomaa and Aly Sabry, later to become a vice president, would be appointed. This was particularly favoured by those who believed Russia was strongly influencing the appointments. As it turned out however, this triumvirate did not eventuate. A belief spread that Gomaa had refused because he was unwilling to give up the Interior Ministry which controlled the intelligence service. Gomaa himself did not allay the rumour that he was to become part of the ruling triumvirate. On referendum day he was asked by a woman reporter as he was leaving a polling booth: "What is this about you being prime minister?"

"Don't listen to rumours," was his advice. But of course this was taken by some to be a cagey political reply. It turned out to be correct advice, however.

The Egyptian method of announcing an appointment was a story in itself. The newspapers, particularly the semi official and influential *Al Ahram*, obtained leaks which made any Western political commentator look amateurish. Two days before Dr Fawzi's appointment as Prime Minister *Al Ahram* carried the following item: "*Al Ahram* learns that President Anwar el Sadat has elected for the post of Prime Minister a prominent personality held in high esteem at the national, regional and international level." The following day *Al Ahram* and *Al Akbar*, another influential newspaper, carried lengthy profiles on Fawzi; *Al Ahram*'s under the headline "The quiet busy man".

They did not mention however that later in the day it would be announced that he was to be Egypt's prime minister.

Fawzi, an esteemed diplomat and minister, graduated from law school in 1923. It was said that his family wished to nominate him for the position of mayor in the local village, Shubra Bakhum, in Menufieh province. But his reply was that his future was in the diplomatic corps and foreign politics. Since 1952 he had taken part in most important agreements and treaties to which Egypt has been a party. He spoke fluent Italian, French, English, Japanese, Greek and Spanish and of course Arabic.

The Sadat and Fawzi team, supported on the international scene by Riad, an impressive man himself, was destined to represent their country in one of the most difficult times in its history. Egypt, despite early doubts, made the transition from government with Nasser and firmly established itself.

There were opinions that the government would be merely a transitionary one which would be replaced or overthrown within six months. After six months this speculation seemed to have been nonsensical. Sadat had clearly established himself, both at home and abroad.

***

The sun was falling at the end of another day in Cairo. Dokki was standing by his chair which was being occupied by his daughter Sabra, who was nursing her baby brother. Hassan had already left for the day having deposited his box of shoe polishes and brushes under the staircase. Mahmoud had passed by with another gas cylinder for someone, but had gone his merry way. Or not so merry perhaps as his tricycle was heavily loaded for his last round of the day. The heat was out of the sun so the laziness of the atmosphere was gone.

Dokki and Sabra just thought. They didn't communicate with each other. They just stared straight ahead. Hakki, the man who looked after the cars in the flats was hosing out the garage and occasionally muttering something to Dokki. But otherwise everyone was minding their own business. The goat had been fed. It was night.

6. Cairo life. Hassan the shoeshiner leaves for Luxor. A frozen peace initiative and build-up of arms

Five men with glazed eyes sat puffing their bubble pipes. They spoke, but only a couple of words: greetings and farewells, but not chat. They sat as they always did, smoking as their fathers had before them. And probably as their sons would sit in the future. Their bubble pipes on the ground beside them in the dirt of the sidewalk, elaborate affairs standing about three feet high, were as traditional as the men who puffed at their tubes. In some, two at least, the bubbles of smoke could be seen making their way through the water captured in the bowl near the base. The men sat by tall, steel-framed and marble-topped tables. Some held water, some Turkish coffee. One man had a scarf wrapped fully around his head. Another wore a felt hat probably to provide protection from the sun. Another went bareheaded. The other two wore turbans. All wore grey suits, shabby and dishevelled. Every now and then a waiter from the sidewalk café would bring more coffee or another coal for a bubble pipe. But no order or command was needed; the waiter knew the men and knew, instinctively it seemed, what they wanted. The day passed puffing.

The men watched the passing city. Buses, old and rambling, overcrowded beyond belief and trams rumbled past carrying men, women and children hither and thither. Cars in various stages of collapse, and a few new ones, made their way up the street as if propelled by the continuous tooting of their horns. Even in impossible jams, the fault of nobody, the horns would continue their merry sound. And merry some were: even playing simple tunes. Children, men and women walked along adding to the passing scene. It was a city true, but nevertheless a man in faded black tunic, turban, and sandals, just had to get his flock of sheep to market and this was the shortest way. So along the footpath ran the sheep and along the road the shepherd followed.

A scruffy and dirty child with a severe mouth malformation asked a foreigner for piasters. The foreigner looking down at the urchin tugging at his trouser leg quickly dug into his pocket drawing out a five piaster note. He half dropped, half passed the scruffy money trying desperately not to notice the fang-like look on the face of the cross-eyed child. Getting the five piasters he scampered off, on to the road and reached his hand into the window of a car driven by another well-to-do victim. A traffic jam, the man could not escape. The performance continued.

A policeman in black serge sat on the step of the gutter and removed his smelly boots. As if by clockwork, he moved his uncoordinated body and faced the east. Then on to his knees he began his homage to Mecca. Traffic jams don't need policemen. They can stay jammed. And the horns can keep honking. The policeman kept praying.

Small shops, resembling cupboards faced the footpaths on either side of the road. In one a carpenter was working on a mock Louis XVI chair. In another a team of busy men were ironing clothes. Every now and then a small boy wearing what appeared to be pyjamas left carrying a board on which a neatly pressed shirt was lying. Down the road he would make his way nodding greetings as he went to the regular bystanders.

Men of every shape and size, dressed in reject khaki military uniforms of still different shapes and sizes, incongruously wore large brass medals on which the words in English and Arabic were written: "Cars Guard". These cars guards managed to park cars one, two, or three deep along the side of the road. All done for a few piasters each. In some roads there were more cars parked than moving and in still others all parked, it seemed.

Past this bustle a man in a striped galabia pushed his way along Sharia 26 July, a street which got its name from the date King Farouk was deposed. It was Hassan. Half walking, half running, he was in an unusual hurry. Past the man pushing his sheep along the footpath; past the cupboard-like shops; past the men drinking Turkish coffee and smoking bubble pipes. Head high in his same characteristic stance, it was as if he was standing still from his waist up, but running from his waist down. Along his long nose he scanned his course. Dodging small boys, old men, a blind man unsuccessfully selling raffle tickets, dogs, cats and bicycles using the footpath instead of the road, he made his way.

He felt exhausted just walking along the street. Oh to be out of Cairo. Then he was at the bridge, also named July 26. The traffic was going the other way so he had to wait for a green light. Then he crossed the road and made for the bridge. The worst was over now. He could walk across the bridge footpath in relative relaxation. Only the occasional donkey, bicycle, tricycle loaded with bananas, or camel dripping green grass from its mouth, caused him to alter his course.

In the opposite direction a man was leading his camel. A giant, old and rangy beast it was. The camel's skin looked like the leather of an old worn out saddle from a horse. The man leading it was small and had a handful of green grass under one arm and the other arm was systematically reaching into the bundle and grabbing a handful. The hand would then reach over his shoulder where the camel's head was going up and down rhythmically as the beast walked. It was almost as if it was some wooden toy, the head of which would nod when a child with fancy magnetic grass enticed it. The giant camel made the man in front look minute. The great steps of the animal made the man look as if he was running on the spot. Past Hassan they walked.

Hassan continued his way. Across the bridge and then once on the other side he took a short cut not wanting to push his way along the busy sidewalk of the continued July 26 street. He turned into a side street and past the big houses of Zamalek, mainly occupied by embassies. On one side of the street were houses facing on to the river. On the other side of the road large blocks of apartments threw continual shadows over the street. Once it must have been a brighter street, but today it looked quite dingy and depressing.

It was a one way road. But one way roads were not taken too seriously in Egypt. The traffic went both ways just the same, in spite of the fact that there were always police patrolling the areas. But the police turned a blind eye. Why not, why confuse the situation by charging the motorist at fault? That would take time and a jam would develop anyway. It would be defeating the purpose. Better to let the motorists solve the problem themselves. But this road was only wide enough for one car at a time, so inevitably a jam was likely to develop every now and then. Like today as Hassan was walking along. A whole stream of traffic was pouring off the bridge and taking the same turn Hassan had taken. They were in the right. The road was one way - their way. It was the other man's fault. He had come out of a side street half way along. He was a taxi driver and was damned sure he was not going to give in. So the horns started honking. No one gave in. Hassan thought that by the Prophet if he had his shoeshine box with him he would be in business. Captive clientele, it was. But he didn't, for he was on his way to Abu el Feda to pick it up from Dokki's.

He continued walking. Then stopped dead. His eyes began to shift in his head. The sound of the horns of the jammed cars was too much for him. It was too good an opportunity. He dug his hand deep into a pocket inside his galabia. And out came a large handkerchief, once white, but now brown with dirt. If he couldn't shine shoes, he could clean car windows, thought Hassan as he approached the nearest car.

"No," waved the driver knowing full well that he would have to pay a couple of piasters if Hassan wiped the window.

"No?" questioned Hassan continuing to wipe the window.

"No."

Hassan then walked to the next car and did the same. A similar response so he moved down the line one car after another. He did not do very well, but then even six piasters was better than nothing. No piasters won, if no battles fought, Hassan thought as he continued his way through the streets of Zamalek.

Through the side streets he made his way continually dodging the traffic. Then he was there.

"Sa'id Hassan," called Dokki down the street as the shoeshiner approached.

Hassan acknowledged, but was too worn out to do much more than wave.

"By the Prophet, you look exhausted. You're sweating."

"Yes." He then recounted the details of his story which were not remarkable, but were better than talking about nothing.

"You're late. It is afternoon already," said Dokki.

"I'm off to Luxor tonight on the train."

"Luxor?" questioned Dokki.

"Yes, Luxor. I have told you I go to Luxor for the winter, haven't I?"

"By God, I think I remember," admitted Dokki. "How long for?"

"For the winter, I come back at the beginning of summer."

"Good," said Dokki.

Hassan then reached under the stairs and retrieved his green box. Then uttered a farewell to Dokki, no different than any other goodbye. No account was made of the fact that he would be away for several months. "Goodbye. See you again. God willing. Inshalah."

"But what about my shoes," said Dokki as he placed his right foot on the shining stand.

"No not today. I'm off to Luxor. I'll miss the train."

Dokki removed his foot reluctantly and repeated his farewell. The two exchanged waves as Hassan walked off up the street the same way he had come. Pushing past the same people he had overtaken earlier in the day Hassan walked along to July 26 Street. But this time he was on the opposite side of the island and making his way to another bridge leading across the other branch of the Nile. Across, he turned and walked back the same way he had come, but on the other side of the river. He was now away from the big houses of Zamalek and into the poor area where houses were small and tumbling down. He fitted more into the scene here, but there was no place for a shoeshiner in the five or ten-piaster category.

On top of these faded and run-down buildings mud shelters were built like beehives on the limbs of trees. Inside these little shelters, lived people. In the heart of Cairo in 1971 lived people on the roofs in mud shelters more fitting for moles than humans. Hassan went his way never noticing, never caring.

The heat was out of the sun by the time he reached the railroad track. There was no station, just a road crossing. A few others were also waiting for the train. On reaching the crossing he put the green box by his side, rested one foot upon the stand, and stood erect, thinking. He looked down the track one way and then the other. But no train was in sight. It had not taken as long as he thought to cross Cairo so he was in good time. It was still light, but the heat was out of the sun and a cool breeze blew across the bare dust on either side of the railway line. Children were playing across the line. Dressed in filthy pyjama-like garments, they looked the same colour as the dusty ground. But were dirtier.

"Hello friend," said Hassan to another man.

A reply came and Hassan added: "Like a shine?"

"No."

"Just a brush then?"

"No."

"Alright friend," said Hassan turning to another man. "Like a shine?" The man said yes so Hassan removed his brushes and rags from the box and began his task. But before he was half finished the train rounded the far corner and headed towards them. "I'll finish them in Luxor," pledged Hassan.

Quickly he packed up his polishes, brushes and rags and grabbed the box by the foot stand which also served as a handle. Again he stood erect and watched the approaching train along his long nose.

A strange place to wait for a train, one might think.

But no, in reality it was very wise. The train was forced to slow down near the crossing for fear of running into children. There were no fences either side of the track at this section and in the past several children had been killed. So Hassan and his friends made use of this caution.

As the train reduced speed they got ready, Hassan with his green box firmly in his hand. The engine of the train had steps near the front and two gangways either side of the body. Perfect for what was about to take place. The first man jumped onto the steps and climbed on to the gangway and then pulled himself up on to the top of the engine which was flat. Another man did the same. But the third man, in his enthusiasm to get aboard before the train picked up speed, bumped into Hassan spilling the polish and brushes from his box.

"By the Prophet . . ." uttered Hassan. But time was too short to continue the curse. He quickly picked up the spilt equipment and stuffed it into the box. Then he hurried off along the track after the train's engine. But the train was picking up speed now and the run was a battle against time. "Wait," yelled Hassan after the train, but to little avail as he knew. Trains did not wait for paying passengers let alone those scrounging a ride on the roof. But he kept running and slowly he caught up to the engine. Past the driver who was watching the proceedings with great interest, but with little sympathy. Hassan ran, stumbling every few paces on the uneven ground. Then the moment came, he had made it. On to the train he jumped and up on to the gangway he pulled himself. The driver honked the horn in innocent congratulation. But the sharp noise startled Hassan and he nearly fell from the gangway again and off the train. But he managed to stay. He pulled himself up on to the roof of the train and sat for a moment gathering his breath. But only for a moment. "Look out" called another man. "Duck your head." Hassan just managed to fall flat before a bridge passed overhead. He was covered in a cloud of smoke confined by the bridge. He continued to lie flat for a time, more from fright than anything else. Then he slowly lifted his head and watched the scene from a sitting position having been reminded there were no more bridges for some time.

The time passed. The train gradually made its way clear of Cairo on its route up the Nile Valley to Luxor. Through little villages it would pass, sometimes slowing down, sometimes stopping completely. Hassan began to feel cold as it was night. Although the days were still warm in Cairo the nights were cold. Hassan sat on the roof of the jolting train and began to wish he had caught a day train. He lay flat finding it not so breezy and not so cold. He balanced his green box of shiners near his head and shut his eyes trying to sleep. But it was too cold and too rough for that.

Only the benefits of winter in Luxor could make the trip worthwhile, thought Hassan. He was making the trip because in winter there were many tourists in Luxor touring the ancient monuments. And hopefully he thought, all would be wearing shoes. What is more with all the dust up there everyone would need their shoes shined every day. Tourists were good for shoeshiners; they paid more not knowing what the currency was worth. But then it worked both ways, there were always those idiots who didn't know what the currency was worth, but gave less rather than more. There was often the humiliating experience of some tourist who wanted a photograph taken while having a shine. But then you got an extra ten piasters at least for that. It was not the first time Hassan had been to Luxor for the winter. He went every year. It was his routine. In summer he cleaned shoes in Cairo and in winter in Luxor. Very good commercial sense it made, thought Hassan.

The train continued its way through the night.

***

The transition had taken place. Egypt had a new Government. Nasser was dead and Anwar el Sadat was president. The initial mourning was over. The tasks of governing the 34 million people were ahead. The war with Israel, forgotten while Nasser was mourned and a new leader found, was back as the major issue. Not an issue which really impacted many of the 34 million people, but the major political issue. No other single issue was more important to Egypt's future than the Israeli crisis.

Sadat, an old soldier himself although now never in uniform, inherited the problem and it was now as much his as it was Nasser's. He had inherited the decisions Nasser had made. He inherited a ceasefire. Nasser had surprised the world by agreeing to it as part of the plan initiated by Mr William Rogers, the United States Secretary of State. The three-month ceasefire which had more than halfway expired when Nasser died had only three weeks to run at the time of the people's referendum. Sadat was immediately in the thick of it.

Nothing much of real value had been achieved by the contacts with Dr Gunnar Jarring, the United Nations peace mediator, who had originally been appointed following the United Nations resolution in 1967. This amongst other things called for withdrawal by Israel from territories she had occupied during the Six Day War. However, the resolution, drafted by the British Foreign Office, was unclear in some respects. The Arabs' reading of it was that it called for withdrawal of Israel from all occupied Arab territories. Israel, on the other hand, claimed it did not specify all the territories. Due to this, and other frustrations, the peace mission under Jarring had never made much progress and Jarring had several times resumed his post as Swedish ambassador in Moscow.

However the Rogers' plan gave hope. Unexpectedly Nasser had gone along with the plan and the ceasefire had started. But during the ceasefire talks were broken off by Israel because she claimed Egypt had broken the ceasefire agreement and was in fact moving missiles supplied by Russia into the standstill zone on the western side of the Suez Canal. Egypt at first categorically denied that she was, but later modified her stand. Mr Riad, the foreign minister, put it like this: "We have not moved any arms into the standstill zone except once. This was done by Egypt because it was understood that each party had the right to move arms from one site to another inside the same zone, and that any commander had the right to guarantee the security of his troops."

Whether Egypt had not violated the standstill agreement is doubtful. The main point was however that Israel broke off contacts with Jarring because of it and the initiative was frozen.

This is what Sadat inherited: a frozen peace initiative and an expiring ceasefire.

Like the Israelis following Nasser's death, there were those in Egypt itself who were uncertain about the future under Sadat. Would he be harder or softer than Nasser? This question was complicated by the fact that the Sadat government had pledged itself to follow the path of Nasser to the letter and to regain all occupied Arab territories.

Some believed that this might be more difficult than it sounded. And that it would cause more problems than if Nasser had been alive. What Nasser may have been able to accept, they might find it hard to justify under the letter of Nasser law. It was generally accepted at the time that had Nasser died a year earlier it would have been difficult for Sadat to agree to the ceasefire and the American peace initiative without losing a great deal of prestige in the Arab world. It would just not have been written in the Nasser law. Sadat's own nationalistic, more than anti-imperialistic (the American, Israeli and British rather than the Russian variety of imperialism, of course!) and his lack of immediate stature at the time of his taking over (which he soon rectified) contributed to the uncertainty. Would he for instance be able to agree to a peace based on incomplete Israeli withdrawal from the occupied Arab territories? Nasser may have been able to, but could Sadat?

But others disagreed with this. They believed that there was a Nasser dictum to justify any move at any time and that Sadat was free to play the game to his own rules.

In the event, after six months the government was not stressing the importance of following the path of Nasser to the letter, but rather placing emphasis on the fact that Nasser had brought them so far since 1952. They were in control.

During the run up to the expiry of the first three-month ceasefire Israel lodged complaints almost daily over Egyptian missile movements. The Egyptian press and radio carried the complaints as if the Israeli leaders were making a fuss about nothing. "Israel lodges 18th complaint" would be the headline. Who, the Egyptian reader might ask, could ever be bothered complaining eighteen times?

Even while still the interim president, Anwar el Sadat was firmly in the thick of the Arab Israeli crisis. On October 7, Mr Riad, the foreign minister, appearing on Egyptian television defied the Israeli allegations of missile movements by Egypt contravening the ceasefire agreement, by declaring that Egypt would not withdraw one single missile backward from the Suez area. He turned from the defensive to the offensive by saying that Egypt would not permit American-made aircraft to fly over the United Arab Republic in a reference to high-flying spy planes used on behalf of Israel. He declared that the missile system was for defence. Re-emphasising that Egypt had not violated the ceasefire, he said that all missiles had been introduced into the canal area before the day set for the ceasefire.

Then he made a declaration that was to be heard many times in the future months, mouthed both by him and Sadat. It was that Egypt would not agree to the provisional ceasefire being turned into a permanent ceasefire because this would be tantamount to surrender. The Egyptian fear was that the Suez border would become accepted by world opinion if the ceasefire was extended and that Israel would always be able to keep Sinai.

Sadat, while still interim president, also emphasised to Mr Eliot Richardson, Nixon's envoy at Nasser's funeral, Egypt's refusal to withdraw one single missile from the front. He also explained that only a clear-cut fixed time for the extension of the ceasefire was acceptable.

On October 12, just three days before the referendum, an interview with Mr Mohammed Heikal, Minister for National Guidance who although unbeknown to the public, had already tendered his resignation to Sadat, was published in *The Times*, London. In this interview, Heikal told Peter Hopkirk that if Britain was desirous of better relations with the Arabs she would be well advised to say what she meant by the phraseology of the 1967 United Nations' resolution which she had drafted. He described the present wording of the resolution as an example of the clever art of phrasing words for which Britain was renowned. He said the Arabs regarded the wording as yet another example of British deviousness for this had given the Israelis a loophole or at least room in which to manoeuvre.

The crux of Heikal's complaint was that the resolution called for withdrawal of Israel from occupied territories. This, the Arabs claimed, meant all occupied territories, whilst the Israelis naturally enough, said it did not stipulate all of the territories.

About this time one of the greatest breakthroughs for Egypt in diplomacy came with the announcement that the United Nations would debate the Middle East crisis following the 25th anniversary celebrations of the U.N. Egypt realised that she would win wide support, but it remained to be seen just how much. America and Israel, also realising the support Egypt would get, immediately began moves aimed at frustrating or at least delaying the debate.

On his arrival in New York, Mr Riad repeated the Egyptian stand. He also asked Dr Gunnar Jarring and the United Nations' Secretary General U Thant to submit a report to the Security Council outlining details of the obstacles confronted by Jarring in the course of conducting his contacts. The Egyptian request was based on the view that although Israel was claiming that she had broken off contacts with Jarring because of Egyptian ceasefire violations, Israel was still the cause of the peace mission breakdown. Egypt hoped the report would show that Israel was merely using the Egyptian violations, which Egypt was denying, as an excuse to break off contacts. It was argued, quite rightly, that it was to Israel's advantage to delay contacts and seek a semi-permanent ceasefire which would be automatically extended time and time again. This would enable Israel to stay in the occupied territories without signing any peace agreement. Conversely, this was Egypt's fear.

On October 19, just four days after his approval by the people, President Sadat told Egyptian armed forces commanders just this. He said Egypt would not accept the freezing of the ceasefire. She would not extend the ceasefire after November 5 unless it was apparent that the contacts with Jarring were moving towards peace which meant the withdrawal of Israeli troops from the occupied territories.

In the event Sadat not only accepted an extension of the ceasefire for another three months after November 5 but also agreed to an additional thirty-day extension after that, taking the ceasefire up to March 7, 1971. Both these extensions were agreed to in spite of the fact that Egypt stated that no real progress had been made by the Jarring Mission. However these extensions proved Sadat as a statesman and a man seeking peace.

A boost for Egyptian diplomatic sympathy came in mid-October when it was disclosed in an American newspaper that the United States was secretly dispatching Phantom jets to Israel during the ceasefire period. Evidently American service pilots were flying the Phantoms to Cyprus where the American colours would be replaced with the Star of David for the final leg to Israel. This, in Egypt's view violated the ceasefire agreement as much as her missile movements. She said that the United States had given her the assurance that no arms would be supplied to Israel during the period.

In his first interview with the world press following his appointment as president, Sadat told C.L. Sulzberger of the *New York Times* that: "Our concept of the policy of non-alignment is that we are for peace and against war, and for freedom and against domination, and for progress and against backwardness, and for the friend and against the enemy."

He said the United Arab Republic would agree to extend the ceasefire for one more period if Israel consented to resume her contacts with Jarring and if the American initiative was carried out in the manner proposed, which called for America to abide by her pledges to Egypt to abstain from supplying Israel with arms including Phantom and Skyhawk aircraft.

Only days later it was announced that the United States was to supply Israel with two hundred tanks and eighteen Phantom aircraft and other military equipment. The tanks were of the most up-to-date M60 type. The same day President Nixon told the United Nations' General Assembly, meeting for the association's 25th anniversary, that the Middle East crisis threatened to explode into a world war. He said that unless the United States and the Soviet Union joined in efforts to avoid war the alternative would be a confrontation with disastrous consequences for the two powers and the world at large. Nixon urged the continuation of the ceasefire after November 5.

Not surprisingly *Al Ahram* commented editorially on October 25: "President Nixon's call for cooperation with the Soviet Union in the international arena on the basis of peaceful competition to head off a third world war is one of the spots of hot confrontation and is inconsistent with America's deeds which make for escalation of the tension to the point of explosion. How can the climate of peaceful competition prevail and how can the factors of world peace be consolidated while the United States is intensifying the conflict in the Middle East by providing

Israel with Phantom aircraft and the United States' armed forces' most up-to-date tanks and sophisticated artillery as part of an incessant flow of military aid to Israel in a deal amounting to $500 million?"

In the meantime the four powers meeting at the United Nations (Russia, France, Britain and the U.S.) had agreed that there was a need to resume the peace mission of Dr Gunnar Jarring and a need to extend the ceasefire arrangements on the Suez Canal front for another definite period, and that the 1967 Security Council Resolution numbered 242 remained the basis agreed upon for any political settlement of the Middle East conflict. The United States was against a formal statement to this effect being released, arguing that a statement to be made by U Thant would be sufficient. The United States evidently also wanted U Thant to include a reference to the alleged violation of the ceasefire arrangements by Egypt, but this was opposed by the other three members of the Big Four.

The United States delegation to the United Nations which was about to debate the Middle East crisis raised a last minute procedural point. In short it was that it was not permissible to convene a meeting of the General Assembly to discuss an international problem while the political committee affiliated to the General Assembly was discussing questions related to world peace. The immediate reaction of Egypt was to contact the chairman of the political committee on the matter and to put forward an official proposal postponing the committee's meetings. She was successful.

Meanwhile with the approaching expiry of the ceasefire, activities on both sides of the Suez Canal were reported to be "feverish". Military commands on both sides instructed their respective forces to be fully prepared for any eventuality.

Coinciding with the start of the U.N. debate, General Ahraraon Yariv, chief of Israeli intelligence, declared at a press conference on October 26 that Egypt had set up one of the strongest networks of missiles in the world which comprised 40 to 50 missiles batteries each made up of some 500 to 600 missiles, one third of which were the SAM 3 type and the rest of the older SAM 2 variety. Egypt did not know whether to take this as a compliment or as evidence that she was really violating the ceasefire as the general claimed that most of these missiles had been moved into the area during the ceasefire.

In his address at the opening of the U.N. debate, Mr Riad, Egypt's foreign minister, reaffirmed his country's determination to liberate every inch of the Arab territory occupied by Israel in the Six Day War. He said that from the moment Egypt accepted the Rogers' peace initiative for a 90-day ceasefire, Israel had frustrated the peace contacts of Dr Jarring. He said that not a single substantive contact was undertaken by Israel. He added that to justify its position Israel had resorted to lies by alleging that Egypt had violated the ceasefire arrangement.

At the United Nations a resolution was drafted by sixteen Afro-Asian countries which called for the resumption of the Jarring mission, another three-month extension of the ceasefire, but denounced the continued occupation of the Arab territories by Israel. America and Israel countered this resolution and submitted another. Mr Charles Yost, the US delegate to the U.N., presented the resolution which called for rectification of the positions arising from the movement of missiles on the Egyptian front in order to bring about the conditions to create the required confidence under which Jarring could resume his contacts. It also called for extension of the ceasefire for another three-month term. Mr Yost further said that the General Assembly would be committing an irresponsible act if it adopted the Afro-Asian draft as it would undermine the accurate balance scored by the 1967 United Nations' Resolution. He was obviously referring to the fact that the 1967 Resolution did not stipulate withdrawal from <u>all</u> occupied territories.

The Israeli Government issued a communiqué the same day which also said that adoption of the Afro-Asian draft would shake the accurate balance established by the 1967 Resolution. It added that adoption would consequently lead to the obstruction of the Jarring contacts, even if the Egyptian missile question was settled. It would also eliminate the progress secured through the American initiative. On the other hand the communiqué described the United States' draft resolution as a natural continuation of the American peace initiative of June 1970.

Another draft resolution composed by several Latin American countries was also submitted. It asserted the 1967 Resolution and then called for resumption of contacts with Dr Jarring and a ceasefire extension of three months.

Before the United Nations voted on any of the resolutions, an unexpected boost for Arab morale came from Britain. British Foreign Secretary Sir Alec Douglas Home urged peace in the Middle East in accordance with the Security Council Resolution of 1967. He believed that Israel should withdraw behind the lines which existed before the Six Day War in 1967. He warned that failure of such a campaign could mean the persistence of the conflict for a further twenty years bringing with it the risk of confrontation between Russia and the US. Needless to say Israel was critical of the statement. However the Foreign Office said that Sir Alec's statement constituted no new plan or proposals for the Middle East crisis. It should not be considered a new initiative but a mere explanation of some ideas about the form and content of the settlement which the British Government had been calling for and upholding particularly within the framework of the four major powers. Nevertheless Israeli-British relations were cooler than they otherwise would have been when Israeli premier Golda Meir arrived in London for talks with Mr Edward Heath, the Prime Minister, a few days later.

On November 4 the United Nations' General Assembly approved the Afro-Asian resolution which rejected the seizure of land by force, provided for a resumption of the Jarring Mission while ignoring the question of military standstill but supporting the extension of the ceasefire for three more months, and asserted the rights of the Palestinians.

The following day Egypt agreed to extend the ceasefire for a further three months after November 5. At this stage she said categorically that she would not under any circumstances agree to a further extension. President Sadat later modified this to a declaration of no extension unless real progress was made by the Jarring Mission during the three-month extension just agreed upon. The resolution passed also called upon the United Nations' Secretary General U Thant to submit a report to the Security Council within two months of the extension on the progress of the Jarring Mission. This, Egypt believed, would prevent the issue being forgotten by the world, and would show Israel up as the frustrating party to the contacts.

Egypt had won a diplomatic battle and was ready to capitalise on the gain. But the passing of the resolution was more notable for what it gave Egypt than what it took away from Israel. Since the creation of the state of Israel in 1948 the membership of the United Nations had greatly increased due to the independence of states in Africa and elsewhere, states which could not be expected to support a nation which was created by countries representing imperialism, the very thing they opposed. However the beginning of a shift of British policy at first publicly indicated by Sir Alec Douglas Home's speech and which was strengthened during the months following the United Nations' approval of the resolution came as a bitter blow to Israel despite the fact that Britain had abstained from voting for the resolution.

7. Hassan the shoeshiner arrives in Luxor. The end of forty days' mourning for Nasser

Dawn was breaking. Hassan shook his head and straightened his wind-tousled hair. But to little avail, the wind just destroyed any semblance of order again. God knows how, but Hassan had managed to get to sleep as the train jolted its clacking way to Luxor. He sat up and surveyed the scene. Across the fields he could see the Nile River flowing in the opposite direction to the train's movement. On either side in the distance he could see the hills of the desert bordering the lush green valley of the Nile. It was still only dawning, but the fellahin were already tending their crops and animals. Along the tracks beside the railway donkeys and camels loaded with all kinds of produce were being led by men, women and children. Age was no bar to work in Egypt.

The sky was blue, creating a contrast with the mud-coloured villages passing periodically on either side of the train. Into one of these small villages the train went, stopping at a siding. On one side of the train a market was operating in the village. Women were sitting like ducks on the ground as if hatching the fruit and vegetables around them. There looked to be too much supply for the demand. But occasionally someone would walk up to one of the vendors and bargain for something, a kilo of oranges or half a kilo of tomatoes. The sight of all that fruit and food roused Hassan's appetite. He had not eaten since Cairo; not since early yesterday in fact. By the

Prophet, no wonder there was a hollow feeling in his stomach, thought Hassan. A man was also selling bread with lentils stuffed inside it. Hassan shouted to him: "Hello friend."

The man looked in the direction of the train and replied: "Sa'id."

"What is the price? How many piasters?"

"Two."

"Bring me one then, by the Prophet."

The man stumbled his way over to the train and Hassan scrambled down the side of the gangway, reached down and took the bread and lentils from the man.

"Thank you," Hassan said as he scrambled up the side of the engine again.

"I said two piasters."

Hassan teased the man and pretended not to hear.

"I said two piasters."

"Here you are my friend. You don't trust me? I trust you my friend." Hassan threw the man a couple of piasters and then began munching his way through the bread. That is good, he thought. He sat cross-legged on top of the train, his green wooden box of shiners in front of him. That is better. Then he began talking to the other men on top of the train.

"It was cold in the night?" questioned Hassan.

"Yes, it was," replied one man.

"Going Luxor?"

"Yes," came the reply.

"And your friend?" Hassan pointed to another man sprawled across the roof.

"He's not my friend."

Hassan persisted: "Your enemy?"

"Not enemy, not friend."

Hassan pondered the reply for a moment and then replied: "But where is he going?"

"Aswan," said the man.

"Ah, Aswan?"

"Yes, Aswan."

"That is good," continued Hassan.

The train slowly started to move again and the market scene passed behind and out of sight. Mud houses with fancy wooden windows and balconies were passed. On the roofs of many of them were built the same mud beehives housing the poorest of the fellahin. Hassan gave the scene no thought, having seen it many times before. He lay down again trying to escape the wind.

Three hours, many villages and much landscape later the train pulled its way into Luxor slowly. As the train lost momentum the noise subsided and Hassan was able to start up his conversation again.

"What is your name friend?"

"Ali."

"Ali? That is good."

"You shine shoes?"

"Yes, want a shine?"

"No."

"No shine? Why not?"

"No."

"But you got shoes, why not have shine. No piasters I clean them for you, my friend for nothing."

"Thanks, that is very kind of you by the Prophet."

"When we get to Luxor. We are nearly there and when we are I will clean them for you. For nothing, my friend."

Noticing the houses of Luxor beginning to gather beside the moving train, Hassan and the others stood up and began to make their way along the top of the train to the back. Every time they came to the end of a carriage they would have to jump the gap to the car behind. Hassan's green box made things difficult. Every time he would hook the bottom of his galabia in his mouth to avoid tripping and hug the box. Then when all was prepared he would do a mighty leap to the next carriage. Easy, he thought, after the first two. The sun was still low in the sky and as they made their way backwards their shadows could be seen clearly above the train's shadow. This fascinated Hassan, but nearly to his detriment. When he had to jump to the next carriage he was so intent on watching his shadow that he nearly missed the carriage altogether. But luckily one foot made it and he fell on to the next carriage. But not without some loss: a tin of black polish fell out of his green box - a day's profit down the drain.

As the train ran into Luxor station Hassan and the others scrambled down a ladder on the back of the guard's van escaping detection. Not that they really had anything to fear as the authorities turned a blind eye, but it was better not to invite trouble, Hassan reasoned.

The man who was going on to Aswan waited under the guard's van during the stop in Luxor. Then he climbed the ladder and made his way along the roof again to the engine. It was warmer there.

How good to be in Luxor, thought Hassan, as he made his way through the streets of the town, swinging his green box as he went. To get some black polish was his aim. No good being a shoeshiner without black polish was it?

When he had transacted his business buying the polish at what he considered a reasonable price, he continued walking to the Savoy Hotel, where he thought he could pick up a few piasters before the morning was out. The Savoy was his first choice because it overlooked the Nile and there you really knew you were in Luxor. The sun lit up the sandy hills on the opposite side of the river past the temples of Thebes. In these hills lay the tombs of countless pharaohs, knew Hassan.

The Savoy Hotel looked just the same when he got there. As it had been since the time of the British and the French, except that new wings had been built in the garden and around the swimming pool. There were about a dozen horse carriages outside waiting to take tourists around the temples.

"Just fifty piasters for the morning all the way to the Karnak temples," called one carriage driver to an American couple who were leaving the hotel.

"Well I say that sounds good," said the man as he helped his wife into the carriage.

"Like a shine before you go?" Hassan questioned trying to make up for the loss of the shoe polish from the train.

"I'm in the carriage now. I'm not going to get out for a shoeshine," called the American as the carriage moved off down the corniche beside the river.

After half an hour Hassan decided he had waited too long for no piasters, so he walked upstream along the river bank to the Luxor Temple. There at the entrance he stopped.

"Like a shine," said Hassan to a tourist who was just leaving.

"No thank you."

"Why not?"

"No thank you very much."

"But your shoes are very dusty."

The man looked down and said: "Yes, thank you very much."

"Like the Luxor Temple?" asked Hassan.

"Yes, thank you."

Then remembering the lines he had found so valuable the winter before: "It is eighteenth dynasty."

"Really?" said the man rather disinterestedly.

"Yes, built mainly by Amenhotep three."

"Really?"

"Yes, see those columns they are forty-two feet."

"Really."

"Why you don't know this? Don't you have a guide?"

"No, I don't have a guide," said the man.

"Would you like me to be your guide?" asked Hassan.

"No . . . La shukran."

"Very good Arabic you speak," said Hassan sarcastically.

"How much is the shine?"

Hassan looked up and gauged the gullibility of the man and then said: "Fifteen piasters."

"Fifteen?"

"Yes," said Hassan as he reached his hand out. When the man handed him the money, Hassan added: "Welcome . . . Welcome to our country."

"Thank you."

***

On November 5, the day following the approval at the United Nations of the Afro-Asian resolution on the Middle East crisis, Egypt commemorated the passing of forty days since Nasser's death. The official mourning period had been forty days, although three days following the death most of the mourning in the streets had stopped. All exhausted after three days of chanting and demonstrating through the streets of the cities and towns, the people had gone home to rest.

On the occasion of the fortieth day *Al Ahram* commented that Abdul Nasser himself would, had he witnessed events after his passing, have appreciated the line of policy the Egyptian people followed. "The Egyptian people have shown deep understanding, rallied around the constitutional institutions left by Abdul Nasser. These institutions are an effective means for continuing the march and a guarantee securing the realisation of the cherished goals and hopes of the departed leader."

On this day several demonstrations of mourning took place in Cairo as the people of Egypt farewelled finally their hero.

8. Ramadan in Abu el Feda. Attempts at Arab federation by Egypt, Sudan, Libya and Syria

Abu el Feda looked the same in spite of Hassan's absence. It was mid-afternoon and clearly-cut shadows were lying across the road. Dokki was sitting in his chair. His son, Sami, was playing in a model car. Sabra was carrying a basket full of beer bottles to some resident who had ordered them. A light breeze was blowing and the felucca men were making use of it. Several boats were sailing on the river. There were only a few cars on the road, but the old red bus excreting voluminous clouds of blue smoke was on its regular run.

Hakki, the man in charge of the garage, walked up on Dokki's beckoning. A smile crept across Dokki's face and he said: "By the Prophet, I'll tell you something. It is now the goat. I think she is to have a family."

"That is good," declared Hakki in surprise.

"Yes, it is good. Very good."

"How?"

"Must have been that goat of Mohammed's. Yes it must have been. About the right time."

"That is good."

The two not satisfied with talking about the goat walked over to the vacant block. The goat was tethered to a tree.

"A fine goat."

"Very fine. You are a lucky man."

"Thank God, I am indeed," said Dokki.

Suddenly a resident called Hakki. He was needed to push a car from the garage so that the resident could get his car out. For this Hakki earned fifty piasters from each tenant each month which added up to about fifteen pounds.

"Coming," he swore more than said.

Dokki kept admiring his prize goat while Hakki hurried to the garage. He would have to build a little house for the goat from mud, he thought. He pondered what he would do with another goat. He could sell it or keep it. Probably better to sell it, but it would be nice to have two goats. But perhaps there would be more than two?

Dokki then returned to his seat just as Mahmoud arrived to deliver some gas to one of the flats. "I tell you Mahmoud I have something to tell you."

"What is that Dokki?"

"My goat, it is having a family."

"A family?"

"Yes."

"That is good, isn't it?"

"Yes it is good. It is very good," said Dokki.

Mahmoud unloaded a gas cylinder and threw it on to his shoulder. He then walked up the stairs into the building. When he returned he was greeted with a question from Dokki.

"Would you like to buy a goat from me."

"By the Prophet I would have nowhere to keep it."

"Nowhere to keep it?"

"No."

Mahmoud then replaced the used cylinder on his tricycle and rode off down the street.

Dokki still smiling from his first attempt to sell a goat not even born sat back in his chair. He looked down at his shoes, saw they were dirty, and thought of Hassan. It would be good to go to Luxor, he thought. But it was good in Cairo also. Better really: better to be in the city. Could not have a job looking after a big block of flats in Luxor: there were no big blocks of flats.

But then if he lived out of Cairo perhaps he could have two or three acres of land and then breed goats for a living. But how would he buy the land? He could save money, but it would take a long time. And was there really any money in breeding goats? He would know the answer to that question when his goat did its bit.

Sabra was struggling down the front stairs with the empty beer bottles having swapped them for full bottles.

According to the Muslim calendar, it was the last day of the eighth month. Tomorrow started the ninth month -

the month of Ramadan when all good and true Muslims fast from dawn to sunset. Dokki was not looking forward to the fasting, but at least at the end of it each day one feasted. And at the end of the month there were four days of feasting.

The sun fell with Dokki still sitting in his chair, Hakki had left an hour or two earlier telling Dokki that there would be a surprise when he returned. Dokki was not over fascinated, wondering what on earth Hakki could do which was surprising. Then he saw Hakki round the corner about two hundred yards away walking towards him. He had something under his arm. What was it? He waited until Hakki was about thirty yards away but still the darkness prevented him from seeing what Hakki was carrying under his arm.

"What is that you have got there?"

"What?" Hakki feigned deafness to continue the surprise.

"By the Prophet it is a dog - a puppy."

"Yes."

"Where did you get it?" Dokki asked.

"By the Prophet my friend who lives in Sharia Ahmed Hishmet gave it to me."

"Gave it to you?"

"Yes, by the Prophet."

"Boy or girl?"

Hakki hesitated and then admitted: "I don't know." Then followed an expert examination of the puppy while it lay legs outstretched on the ground.

Then Dokki pronounced: "Well, I think it's a girl."

"That is good," Hakki said.

"Why is it good? In a year you will have many dogs the way they breed."

"I'll sell them."

"Sell them? Who to? Your friend had to give his away."

Hakki pondered. Dokki had a point. "I'll wait until the time comes." Hakki moved off into the garage with his new possession. He prepared a place for it to sleep in a cardboard box near where he slept on the floor. He put an old hessian bag in the box to make it warmer.

Dokki followed Hakki and watched the proceedings. "Is he Muslim?" joked Dokki.

"Born into a Muslim family, so he is Muslim," Hakki replied.

"Will he fast during Ramadan?"

"Children are exempt, so I suppose puppies are also."

Dokki wandered away smiling. Hakki patted the puppy on the head, settled it into the box, and followed Dokki out of the garage. But the puppy followed.

"You will have to tie the dog to the box, Hakki," said Dokki. Hakki agreed. He lifted the puppy up by the scruff of the neck and returned it to the garage. He found a piece of old rope which he tied around its neck at one end and at the other he secured a knot to a nearby drainpipe. Hakki then left to talk to Dokki. The puppy began to bark.

"By the Prophet, that dog will keep me awake," Dokki said.

"God willing. Inshalah."

Attracted by the barking, Dokki's children arrived on the scene. Sabra and Sami ran to the puppy and patting its head asked: "Whose dog is this?" Hakki said it was his.

"What is its name?"

Hakki did not answer, not having thought of a name, not having even thought of the problem of a name.

"Yes, Hakki what is the puppy's name," asked Dokki?

"It hasn't a name yet," said Hakki.

"Well it's Muslim, call it Mohammed after the Prophet," suggested Dokki.

"But it's a girl. You can't call a girl puppy Mohammed," Hakki pointed out.

No name could be decided upon so the dog, at least for the time being, was going to remain merely The Dog or The Puppy.

The night hours passed. The stillness after midnight was only occasionally interrupted by the tooting of a horn. Across the river however, donkey carts were clipping their clopping way along the road. Loaded with vegetables from the farms outside Cairo they were on their way to the markets and fruit shops of the city. All through the night they continued their routine journeys. Some were loaded completely with cabbages, some with lettuces, still others with a variety of produce. The men driving the carts were well rugged up against the cold night air. Old blankets covered their striped galabias.

Morning came soon enough. At four o'clock a giant blast rang the air. Dokki awoke with a start. He gathered his thoughts and realised that Ramadan had begun. It was the Ramadan gun signifying the beginning of the first day's fasting. Every day for the month a gun would signify the first light of the day and another the falling of the sun. Between the two no food could be eaten. Dokki laid his head down again. Already he felt hungry.

***

Less than a month after becoming president of Egypt, Sadat agreed with President Gaafar Nimeiry of Sudan and Colonel Moammer Gaddafy of Libya, to a plan for federation of the three countries. This decision was the result of a summit meeting held in Cairo which was convened under the Tripoli Charter signed on behalf of Egypt by Nasser on December 27 1969. The federation agreement was to most a surprise, coming so soon after the death of Nasser and even after the signing it was unclear to senior members of at least one of the delegations what it involved.

The agreement, as outlined in a communiqué issued by the three leaders at the conclusion of the summit, called for the establishment of the federation with one political leadership. This, as it transpired, meant a joint political leadership comprising the three leaders themselves.

Some clarification on what the agreement really meant came from the Egyptian Prime Minister, Dr Fawzi, two days later. He told a gathering of Arab ambassadors in Cairo that the agreement between Egypt, Libya and Sudan was neither unity nor federation, but was the first step on a long, long path to federation.

Al Ahram commenting editorially wrote: "There is no doubt that the agreement concluded between the United Arab Republic, Sudan and Libya to set up a federation of the three countries to serve as a nucleus for Arab unity is a great step forward consolidating the Arab liberation movement and the Arab progressive regimes against attempts of encirclement engineered by the imperialistic forces in complicity with international Zionism to stem the Arab revolutionary tide at a time when the Arab nation has lost a man whose mere presence at the head of the Arab struggle was a symbol of its unity."

It went on: "The move embodies the profound awareness of the three revolutions, owing to several geographical, political and intellectual factors, of their historical responsibilities of playing a pioneering role in confirming the concept of Arab unity as a supreme and strategic objective."

The agreement seemed to have been encouraged by Moammer Gaddafy of Libya, a passionate believer in Arab unity and worshipper of the later President Nasser. Gaddafy was a fanatic in some respects. He had banned the sale of alcoholic liquor in Libya since coming to power in a revolution overthrowing King Idris in September 1969. He also converted street signs to Arabic, without sub-titles, and in public buildings it was sometimes difficult to get anyone to speak anything but Arabic. He believed that Arabic was the natural tongue of the people of Libya and that foreign languages merely represented the imperialism and colonialism under which Libya suffered for so long. He lacked the good sense of either Nasser or the more recent revolutionary leader Gaafar Nimeiry of Sudan. A Lebanese friend described him as a "foolish boy". That was probably not an entirely unfair description of the Libyan president who at the time was in his late twenties - the same age as several student leaders throughout the world.

The Egyptians were more cautious for several reasons, not the least their memories of previous ill-fated attempts at Arab unity. Like Gaddafy, Arab unity had been Nasser's dream, a dream which diminished in strength as the years progressed and he saw the difficulties of such unity. In 1958 Nasser and Shuri al Quaitly of Syria signed an agreement forming the United Arab Republic. Mainly due to Nasser's and Egypt's domination of the government of the Republic and their keenness on moving the machinery of government to Cairo it broke apart again in 1961. Although the United Arab Republic involving Egypt and Syria lasted only three years, Egypt retained the name and her flag retained two stars.

Two years later in 1963 another union was set up by Egypt, Iraq and Syria. This, proposed by Syria, was a plan to adopt a common foreign policy and a unified system of defence. This was a looser arrangement than the previous United Arab Republic but met with little more success.

Even in Sudan, Nasser had previously left harsh feelings when in the 'fifties he appeared to encourage union between Egypt and Sudan. This undid much of the good feeling he had created in Sudan by renouncing King

Farouk's designs on the southern neighbour. But any bad feeling held by the Sudanese was forgotten during successive governments and finally during the revolution of May 1969 when Nimeiry came to power.

Broadly speaking the agreement to federate was not unnatural as all three countries had similar revolutionary governments and the geographical positions of the three countries situated side by side made more sense than previous attempts at Arab unity. At the time the idea seemed to be that the three countries could complement each other economically and socially. Libya could provide the finance for development from her multi-million dollar oil supplies, the Sudanese could, if properly developed, supply the skilled labour lacking in both the other two countries.

In years to come it might seem strange that Libya was the one to push the formation of the federation for it would seem that in the long run she had the least to gain. It would be her money which would have to be used for any joint development and this money could be just as well spent solely within Libya. She of course needed expertise and Egypt would provide this. But Egypt would have been prepared to provide expert labour, federation or no federation, to rid her of one of her own major problems: a glut of trained men and women.

The geographical argument for such a federation dissolved within a few months of the federation agreement being signed in Cairo when Syria became the fourth signatory. This was arranged following a coup in Syria overthrowing Dr Atassy. One of the first foreign policy moves of the new Prime Minister Hafez el Assad was to explore the possibility of joining. The Egyptian government found it difficult to hide its pleasure at the overthrow of the extreme Baath Party regime under Atassy. This and the three leaders' genuine desire for Arab unity, together with the military advantages for Egypt, overrode the geographical disadvantage and Syria was declared a member. But nevertheless the original neat and compact unity lost something with the addition of the state of Syria on the other side of Israel.

Shortly following Syria's joining the federation it was strongly rumoured that should the two Yemens achieve their attempted link-up they too would wish to join the now quadripartite federation. However moves in this direction were taking longer to materialise.

The military advantage of Syria's joining was obvious. For a long time the Arab eastern front against Israel of Syria, Lebanon and Jordan had been uncoordinated and weak. So diminished in strength was it that it could not even pretend to be a threat to the enemy, although the Palestinian resistance did carry out considerable harassment from these territories. The thing that Egypt needed most at this time of peace negotiations and mounting tension was the moral support of a strong eastern front. Syria could now form the crux of just that sort of front.

Immediately following the coup in Syria and the emergence of Hafez el Assad, General Mohammed Fawzy, Egypt's War Minister, was dispatched to Damascus. This was the first of many military meetings to follow in the coming months and the first steps towards coordination of the military command were taken at this early meeting.

One rather pertinent question arose. How much sharing of military equipment and men would take place within the federation? In reality it now appeared that there would be very little real commitment to Egypt by either Libya or the Sudan in men or equipment from these two countries not bordering on Israel. Sudan for one thing was too busy with its own problems in the southern provinces where separatist forces were trying to create a separate state in the three most southern provinces from the more developed northern provinces. But the question arose as to whether the Libyans would allow Egypt to make use of her Mirage fighters? The answer was yes, but the fact was that they would be no use to Egypt: she already had her own aircraft, but not enough pilots.

So what was created was an agreement to work towards a federation which was to everyone's account a long way off. When the leaders held another summit meeting in January 1971 - this time with Syria as well - also in Cairo, it appeared that the agreement had merely created a forum to allow the discussion of topical Arab matters. Although this summit had been convened to discuss mainly commercial topics, the main discussion was over renewed fighting in Jordan between the authorities and the resistance. The approaching expiry of the Middle East ceasefire on February 5 was the other main topic. As a side point to this Gaddafy, not satisfied with the four power Arab summit, proposed a full Arab summit involving countries from Morocco to Iraq. But this, due to lack of enthusiasm on the part of most countries never did eventuate.

It seemed for a while that the Libyans and the Sudanese, neither having a border problem with Israel, were being more loud-mouthed over the Middle East crisis than Egypt herself. Both Gaddafy and Nimeiry appeared to be making more hard-line statements than Sadat. Nimeiry said that he hoped and was sure that the November 1970 extension of the ceasefire would be the last. And Gaddafy seemed to spend much of his time talking about Pan-Arabising the conflict, much to the Saudi Arabians', Kuwaitis' and Lebanese disinterest; those three countries being more interested in satisfying themselves with token commitments to the battle.

Although the Libyan leadership was extremely keen on the idea of federation, there were whispers of discontent both from that country and Sudan. The main worry seemed to be over the fact that Egyptian experts might take the place of Libyans and Sudanese. It is true that at that time both countries needed the help of some expertise, but with accelerating education schemes the need might be overcome at least partially. Would then these two countries find that their prime jobs were being held by Egyptians?

The other fear was that Cairo would, if the federation eventuated, tend to take over the political leadership. Only time would tell, but at the time Sadat and the Egyptian officials were treading very carefully. Certainly no forecast could be made at that time.

The Sudanese particularly were being very careful to point out that the agreement so far was merely the first step towards federation. Whether it was historical, or just fear of being submerged beneath the oil-rich Libya and the politically-strong Egypt, the Sudanese I spoke to were extremely reluctant to tread too fast along the road to federation. However they, even more than Egypt, needed finance to help development of their vast areas of desert and parched land, much of which would be irrigated from the Nile and made extremely productive. Already one major scheme, the Gezira Scheme, was doing just this thanks to British help. But Sudan knew she did not need Libya's help to develop her country. Although Russia was showing some reluctance due to her already giant expenditure further downstream on the Nile, China was all too willing and had already started making extremely large contributions. When in the Sudan I saw some women soldiers wearing what looked like Chinese-style uniforms. I asked my Sudanese friend where they had come from. He laughed and admitted: "China". They looked rather incongruous beside the spick and span uniforms of the men - another benefit from the days of British influence.

The most fascinating question which arose over the proposed federation was whether or not the agreement would have been signed so soon had Nasser lived? If it had been Nasser and not Sadat it could be argued that neither Nimeiry nor Gaddafy would have wanted to jump headlong into an agreement which would endanger their power. Nasser had shown in the past that when such an agreement was signed it was not long until he started moving the power to Cairo under his wing. This is precisely what happened in the ill-fated 1958 union with Syria. This could have been felt all the more by Gaddafy and Nimeiry, both relative newcomers to political leadership. But with Anwar el Sadat things were different. If there had been a fear with Nasser, it did not exist with Sadat. He was also a newcomer. He was also feeling his way. Speaking to some senior Sudanese I asked them whether they believed that the federation would have taken place so soon had Nasser lived? They replied that had it not it would have been because of Nasser's caution. They believed he would have stepped extremely carefully having been burnt before. They are probably right - bearing in mind both Gadaffy's and Nimeiry's respect for Nasser.

It is worth noting that although the federation was well under way neither Nimeiry, Gaddafy nor Assad attended the opening of the High Dam at Aswan by Sadat and Soviet President Nikolai Podgorny. This seemed surprising as the High Dam was surely the greatest single achievement of post-revolution Egypt and a benefit one would assume to the federation as a whole. All the leaders had announced their intention to attend some time before the event was held, but on the day it was merely Sadat and Podgorny.

Even as early as this it seemed that the federation was getting further away, not closer. It would serve to promote a focus for the Arab nation as a whole but whether firstly, it would materialise, and secondly, it in reality would serve as the nucleus for further real Arab unity seemed extremely doubtful. Nasser would have done well to be cautious. His fingers had been burnt before.

9. Provocation along the Suez Canal and Egypt's diplomatic offensive. Bairam feast – the end of Ramadan in Abu el Feda

The Muslim month of Ramadan was always a test in patience. By afternoon Muslim tempers were frayed and the last hours to breakfast were merely moped away. And the more the month progressed, the more agonised the Muslim faces became. So perhaps it was not surprising to hear in late November the Tel Aviv allegations of Egyptian reconnaissance flights over Israeli Suez Canal emplacements. It was the last week of Ramadan and the Egyptian government, quite plainly, was impatient.

Impatient because with the first months of the extended ceasefire nearly over, the Israelis were still quietly digging their secure lines - and what is more probably starting their working day with a gigantic meal. Impatient because with only two months of the ceasefire left, Israel was no closer to the Jarring talks table and the host himself had resumed duties as Swedish ambassador in Moscow.

The Egyptians knew the Israeli game, they said. "America and Israel want to keep the ceasefire up on a regular basis with Israel staying on the eastern bank of the Suez Canal," said President Anwar el Sadat. It made some sense: why should Israel sign a formal peace agreement involving the return of most occupied territories?

It appears that the Cairo government felt that something was needed to jolt the Israelis back to the peace table.

Nothing could have been more suitable than a series of reconnaissance flights, not the high-flying kind, but the more down-to-earth variety which would make the teeth of the Israeli soldiers chatter. The Egyptians followed this act with an elusively diplomatic statement neither confirming nor specifically denying the missions.

Within a few hours an Israeli command spokesman was commenting that the missions "create a grave situation in the Suez Canal front". And within twenty-four hours reports from Tel Aviv were indicating that the return-to-Jarring faction within the Israeli cabinet was gaining support. It appeared that if the Egyptians had held a plan to hot up the truce in an effort to get Israel back to Jarring they had at least had some success.

About the same time Egypt complained to Washington about United States reconnaissance missions in high-flying aircraft over Egyptian territory. The Egyptian overflying may have been designed to put pressure on Israel and the United States to stop their missions. However complaints by both sides - from Israel about the Sokhois and from Egypt about the American high-fliers - seemed to fall on deaf ears and both reconnaissance missions were continued, the Egyptians' more blatantly.

During the next months the overflying in Egyptian Russian-built aircraft continued along the Suez Canal. In spite of the fact that American high-flying reconnaissance planes had been flying well into Egyptian airspace, the Egyptian overflying looked like a dangerous game to be playing. As the scheduled expiry of the ceasefire on February 5 came nearer speculation began as to what the consequences might be if the overflying continued once the ceasefire lapsed. Although mere speculation, military attachés at the western embassies seemed to be in accord in thinking that the planes might not get the full length of the canal.

The fascinating thing about the overflying was that the Sokhoi was not a good aircraft for reconnaissance missions as cameras were not easily fitted. This raised the belief that the missions might be purely target practice for the SAM missiles. The SAM 3, the later and more sophisticated Russian-supplied missile in Egypt's possession, could have easily been tested with the help of these flights. The main trouble with the defensive missile system at that time was that it was only operative in theory. The overflying would have enabled the crews to lock the radar of the missiles on to their own planes as they swept along the canal at about the same height, speed and position as an Israeli air attack might be expected. Since the ceasefire had begun there had been few, if any, Israeli aircraft in that area flying at that low altitude and the Egyptians may merely have been in need of some practice. Whether or not this was the sole reason for the overflying seems doubtful, but the missile crews are sure to have made use of the opportunity.

Whether the overflying had anything to do with Israel's decision to contact Jarring nobody can say with certainty. Probably not, but it was important for the Egyptians to maintain the belief throughout the world that the Middle East crisis was near exploding. The danger was that all would be quiet in the second term of the ceasefire leaving the world to believe that perhaps the crisis was over and that Israel really did belong in Sinai and the other occupied territories.

It was with the realisation of the importance of world opinion in mind that during the second ceasefire period Egypt launched a massive and comprehensive diplomatic drive throughout the world, dispatching senior officials to world capitals. She wanted to continue the considerable advantage she had achieved when the United Nations' General Assembly approved the Afro-Asian drafted resolution - the draft most favourable to her.

President Sadat's plan was for a diplomatic offensive in the international as well as the Arab sphere and aimed at making Egypt's stand quite clear before the expiry of the ceasefire due on February 5, 1971. The aim was to point out to world leaders that Egypt had done her utmost in the field of quiet diplomacy to settle the Middle East crisis on the basis of the Security Council Resolution of 1967 and the October 1970 Resolution. The idea was also to point out that Egypt would not extend the ceasefire along the Suez Canal again.

The first delegations to be dispatched were under the leaderships of the two vice presidents, Hussein el Shafei and Aly Sabry. Shafei was to go to Yugoslavia and Sabry to Moscow. Mr Mahmoud Riad was sent to several West European countries including Britain. Other delegations strategically covered the world.

This diplomatic campaign continued right up until the date set for the expiry of the ceasefire. But while stressing that it preferred peaceful solutions to the crisis, Egypt was also making the point that it would not hesitate to pursue the military course to achieve Israeli withdrawal from the occupied territories. Continually Sadat, Dr Fawzi the prime minister, and other cabinet ministers were declaring that Egyptian troops were at the high alert and ready to face battle should it come. On the last day of November 1970, President Sadat addressing soldiers on the front along the Suez Canal said that the Armed Forces were capable and prepared for battle and that they were prepared to win the battle. He also declared that Egypt would not withdraw a single missile and not cede an inch of Egyptian soil, making an obvious reference to the occupied territories.

This talk of war by the Egyptian leaders was not all aimed at the ears of the world. It was aimed at home as well as a morale booster for the people who had never quite recovered from the Six Day War defeat in 1967 and who, if not shortly going to be asked to fight another war, were being at least asked to consider war as a possibility. It had the desired effect. By the time the February 5 expiry date came around many Egyptians, informed and educated ones included, were quite confident about the outcome of any war and although would not welcome it, would believe it a rightful course to follow against the Israelis.

In fact the high morale at the time of the ceasefire expiry on February 5 and during the next months caused Sadat some worries. When he extended the ceasefire for a further thirty days and when no concrete advance towards a permanent peace came from Israel, Egyptians were beginning to ask why the Army was not crossing the canal and retaking the lost territories. If the army is so capable why then are they not getting into action? In fact Mohammed Heikal at one stage questioned in *Al Ahram* the strength of the army and pointed out that any battle would not necessarily end in Egyptian victory. This, if not inspired or approved by Sadat, certainly would not have been unwelcome to the Egyptian president. It clearly helped him keep the masses happy with his balancing of the delicate peace during the official and unofficial ceasefires.

Against the Israelis, yes, but what the Egyptians would think worth fighting for was another matter. Although the Egyptian masses during this period as always since 1967 were told that a rightful and honourable solution would be nothing short of total withdrawal of Israel from the occupied territories, most Egyptians had no direct interest in the occupied territories except that their occupation meant the closure of the Suez Canal. They would of course be prepared to fight, but whether they would be prepared to fight all the way to the pre-1967 borders (leaving completely alone the question of whether they would be capable of it anyway) is another matter.

The regaining of morale by the Egyptians was not entirely due to good public relations and publicity. Since 1967 the armed forces due to Russian aid had been completely rebuilt and were in fact far superior to what they were before the war. Also a change in conscription regulations meant that only young men of a fairly high educational standard were being admitted, thus closing the gulf between the officers and men which existed in 1967 to the detriment of Egypt.

Not surprisingly a report by the commanders of the armed forces presented to President Sadat supported the confidence in the forces. The report confirmed that the forces had completed the target set for the year as part of the rehabilitation scheme following the Six Day War. It also stated a fact that was already assumed which was that the Egyptian force had benefitted from the ceasefire in that it enabled them to step up combat efficiency and build up equipment.

However Mr Riad, foreign minister, judging from his statements was taking a gloomy view of the situation although it could be assumed that he was at least partly directing his words at the world for diplomatic advantage. With the ceasefire period nearing its end and Israel still not contacting Dr Jarring, and Egypt having already declared that "real progress in the peace mission was a precondition for a further extension", Mr Riad said: "Israel will pretend to contact Jarring a short time before the date fixed for Jarring to make his report to the Security Council so that she may appear before the world as if she were respecting the United Nations resolution. But afterwards she will place obstacles and stall to render contacts useless. The aim of this old manoeuvre is to gain time until the ceasefire deadline expires at the times these fictitious contacts are still on. America will then propose an extension of the ceasefire for a new period and thus freeze the situation. Israel will benefit by stabilizing occupation and turn it into an accomplished fact."

In the event Israel did agree to contact Jarring just before U Thant reported to the Security Council. America did propose an extension of the ceasefire. The contacts were still going but to little avail when two months later Egypt agreed to extend the ceasefire while stating that no progress had been made. Mr Riad had been dealing with the Arab-Israeli dispute for a long time.

***

The Ramadan gun blasted its last blast for the year: the month of fasting was over. Ahead there were four days of feasting. Dokki as usual was up with the sun for the first full day of feasting. It was Bairam.

Dokki wore a jet black galabia with white lining, a garment kept only for the Muslim feast days of the year. His children were also dressed up in their best clothes, the girls in red stockings and red and blue matching dresses. The little boy was dressed in grey trousers with a Fair Isle-type jumper. Anyone could tell it was a special day.

Throughout the Muslim world men, women and children were exchanging greetings and expressing pleasure in the fact that the month of fasting was over - and the days of feasting started. In Abu el Feda the scene was no exception. Everyone was shaking hands with everyone. One did not have to know anyone to confidently shake the hand of every other passer-by. Everyone was munching something. Everyone was breaking the fast.

Along the road rumbled a hand-pushed canteen brightly coloured from which cakes and pastries and every describable sickly and sweet food were being sold. The man pushing was being followed by a stream of children and their parents. He was an Arab pied piper. The children were persuading their parents to buy them a treat and their parents were indulging. Everyone was breaking the fast.

For foreigners the greeting was "Merry Christmas" as those two words, thought the Arabs, came pretty close to what it is all about. It also had the side effect of stimulating any little hand-out from the foreigner who might otherwise not understand the full meaning of the feast. Perhaps not the meaning meant by the Prophet Mohammed, but then religion has to move with the times and needs of the people.

Children were riding bicycles. They had specially decorated them for the day by threading coloured streamers of paper through the spokes in the wheels. As they rode along the effect was a coloured kaleidoscope as the colours ran into each other. The children were continually ringing the bells on the handle bars and the adults were continually tooting the horns of their cars.

No-one was wearing their normal clothes - except of course the very poor. The pyjama-clad children had miraculously disappeared from the scene and a whole nation of neatly dressed people had taken their place. It was a day to be proud.

It was a day of treats for the children. In Cairo parents were taking them to parks where they rode in horse-drawn carriages with other children. It was a treat and a tradition. Every year the children of Cairo gathered in a park near the Gezira Sporting Club on the island of Zamalek. And every year all the horse carriages of Cairo would gather to take the singing children through the streets.

Parents sat munching sweetmeats while their children went in the carriages. A happy day was had by all.

As night fell they headed for home, greeting everyone on the way. Eating more as they wound their way through the streets cluttered with honking cars.

But in Abu el Feda the day was not so special for Hakki who had spent it pushing cars out of the garage enabling other cars to be driven away. The residents tossed Hakki another couple of piasters because it was Bairam. He was not dressed in anything special. He was in his same galabia. It seemed nothing special for him this day except even for Hakki it meant the end of a month of fasting which he had observed. His small dog started to yap as it sat in its cardboard box. Dokki, his children and Hakki exchanged greetings despite the fact that they had already done so before. It was a good day for shaking hands. It was a day for greetings. Dokki and his family had also spent the day at home. They had dressed up in their best clothes, but they spent the day as always.

The little girl Sabra walked to the little dog and leaning over shook the dog's front paw as if as a handshake: a Bairam greeting. Then the little boy followed his sister and repeated the gesture. Hakki smiled as the little dog yapped for more attention.

"He wants a Bairam greeting from you Dokki," laughed Hakki.

"Does he indeed by the Prophet," Dokki then moved over to the little dog's box and shook the front foot of the puppy. "There you are Hakki, a greeting."

The children bubbled with excitement and Sabra ran off to her mother who was preparing the evening feast to get an extra morsel of food for the puppy to make the day just a little bit different. She ran back with a small piece of meat and some bread dipped in stock.

"The dog likes that Sabra by the Prophet," said Hakki.

"So he should. That is good meat specially for the feast," remarked Dokki.

"Less for you won't hurt you Dokki," continued Hakki.

The children then ran out of the garage and continued their game with the model car. "I'll push you. You hop in," said Sabra to her brother. They kept on until the feast was ready.

Hakki and Dokki continued talking. They thought of Hassan in Luxor, but not for long. They thought of their stomachs as the man with the canteen made his way past again. They indulged in another cake before the feast was ready. It was a day of celebration.

10. A shoeshiner's life in Luxor. Government at work in Egypt

Up early at the crack of dawn and to bed when the sun falls, that was the secret of life. After dark no-one needed shoes shined because no-one could see if they were clean or not, knew Hassan all too well. He stretched his arms out as the sun rose above the desert, wiped his eyes, and jumped rather shakily to his feet. Another day, another dawning, more shoeshines, and hopefully more piasters, thought Hassan. His friend was still asleep beside him. His friend had agreed to let Hassan sleep the night in return for cleaning his shoes. So Hassan quietly went about the task giving the shoes a bright shine. He left them near the face of his friend so that it would be a nice surprise when he awoke: shiny shoes for a bright new day. Then out the door Hassan went.

There was light dew on the ground causing the dust on the road to cling to Hassan's sandals and feet. It was not the dirt that was worrying him, but the cold. His feet felt like ice. Only a few people were up and the street outside was nearly deserted. Most of the small shops still had their shutters up. The sun was not yet high enough in the sky and long shadows reached across the street. It was cold although the sky was clear blue.

Hassan saw a man tending the fire in a portable canteen kitchen. How nice something warm to eat would be. He focused on the man trying to see whether he was wearing shoes or not: dirty shoes or not. He was: a good start.

Hassan quickened his speed a little as he approached the canteen along the dirt road.

"Hello friend," said Hassan.

"Hello, how are you?"

The greeting went to seemingly interminable lengths before the two got down to transacting business.

"That smells good by the Prophet," said Hassan pointing to the display of stews and rice the man was stirring in the brightly coloured mobile canteen.

"It not only smells good, by the Prophet," replied the man.

"That is good."

"Pigeon and rice, it is," said the man.

"Really, pigeon and rice," said Hassan more as a statement than a question.

"Yes, pigeon and rice."

"That is good, friend . . . Friend, want a shine? Your shoes are a little dusty. Like a shine?"

"No . . . la."

The conversation lagged a little and then Hassan said: "No charge for a friend. I'll clean them for no piasters."

The man agreed and Hassan started cleaning the shoes. "That really smells good," said Hassan desperately not wanting the conversation to lag.

"My friend, would you like some pigeon and rice?"

"No."

"No?"

"No, I'm very poor."

"For you friend, no charge."

"By the Prophet that is kind of you."

Hassan ate his breakfast continually enthusing about the food. Then he farewelled the man and headed off down the road towards the river.

Slowly the shutters were coming off the shops revealing every describable article. The shops here also were like cupboards in a wall. Hassan stopped at an open door. There down a couple of steps inside three men were busily ironing clothes. The irons were exchanged every now and then as they lost their heat. For this task a small boy was needed to run the cold irons to the fire replacing them with freshly heated irons. This same small boy would also do the delivery. He would go to the houses round about picking up washing and delivering neatly ironed clothes later in the day. They were at work early. Already the smell of steam surrounded the room. Hassan passed the time with the men enquiring by the way whether they would like a shine. The owner of the shop said yes, but the others declined.

Further along the road a man was opening his bicycle shop. He had a good trade hiring bicycles to tourists. Hassan could never understand it. People with all the money in the world would come to Luxor to ride bicycles. They would come on giant aircraft and then ride bicycles. It just did not make sense, he thought.

"Like a shine," he asked the man. The man agreed and Hassan settled down to the task. "These are good shoes," said Hassan.

"Yes they are very good . . . very expensive."

Hassan nodded amazed by the obvious wealth of this man who hired bicycles to wealthy tourists. He deserved his money though; it can't be an easy living persuading rich men and women to ride bicycles. But it seemed to be easier than persuading rich men and women to have their shoes shined. The ironies of life, thought Hassan.

The man tossed Hassan two piasters. Hassan struck a mean look. Wealthy as he was, he was mighty mean with piasters. Sweat your hands out all day cleaning the shoes of your countrymen for little reward: better to concentrate on the tourists, thought Hassan. Pocketing the two piasters and uttering the words "thanks friend", Hassan continued his way to the Luxor Hotel. There a shoeshine is worth more than a mean two piasters.

***

The amazing thing, though, was not the speed with which the government under the leadership of Sadat and the premiership of Dr Fawzi got back to fighting the crisis with Israel both diplomatically and with the help of the media, but the speed with which it started dealing with the really pressing problems of the Egyptian masses. Although proper judgement could not be made in 1971 on the social and home affairs decisions they made in the first months in office because not enough time had elapsed, it was clear that the government was making an all-out drive to help the people.

This was probably one of the greatest points in favour of the decision by Sadat, and one assumes other senior Egyptians, to form a collective government. Turning back to the nomination speech to the National Assembly, Sadat said: "It is not in my capacity, nor in the capacity of any one person to shoulder all the burdens the late president had assumed." Although it would still be sacrilege to say it in Egypt, it appeared by the rapidity with which the new government tackled these problems that it may have been even too much for Nasser. A great deal was obviously in urgent need of attention. Although to be fair, the early social decisions of the new government were all couched in the statement that they were following the wishes of the late president. Nevertheless, the great thing about the collective government which included as well as Sadat and Fawzi, the four deputy premiers, was that it enabled whole sectors of the government to be allotted in theory at least to a government official capable of making decisions without continual reference to the President. Unlike the virtual one-man rule of Nasser it allowed all sectors to be carried on at one time. This division of labour probably contributed to the undoubted progress Egypt made on the foreign side as well as her progress at home.

On October 22, 1970 just seven days after the people's referendum and even before the new cabinet had been formed, the last Nasser cabinet met under the new prime minister and considered mainly improvement of government services to the people. This involved sewage and water supply as a means of encouraging public cleanliness and health. The new National Guidance Minister Mr Mohammed Fayek (he had replaced Mr Mohammed Heikal) said afterwards that the cabinet had considered these questions for the sake of continuity. They had been dealt with at the last cabinet meeting attended by Nasser. Even at this first meeting the cabinet considered improvements to the appalling transport system in Cairo and the other main cities, and ways of lifting the consumption of consumer goods and the provision of such goods.

For anyone who had ever lived in Cairo the attention given to the water supply and sewage services was greatly appreciated. In the Egyptian capital no-one could live without a rubber plunger which had to be used at least monthly and often more frequently to clear blocked lavatories and drains. The water service also could tend to be unreliable, always giving out on cold winter's mornings when one was under a hot shower or even worse when one's wife was enjoying a hot shower.

The same day President Sadat told Egyptian governors at a swearing in ceremony at the Kubbeh Republican Palace to communicate with the people in their own governorates to find out about the people's problems and hopes. He added that they should work towards overcoming all obstacles in the way of solving these problems. Sadat said: "I am convinced that no work is done, and no effort is made without mistakes. But I believe at the same time that there is a great distinction between a mistake arising from honest work aimed at solving the problems of the people and fulfilling their hopes and a mistake made as a result of carelessness, fatalism, wilfulness. I am ready to take part, at any time and with all efforts, in solving any problems that may prove difficult after you have studied it with the Prime Minister and the Minister for Local Government."

Two days later, on October 24, 1970 Sadat and Dr Fawzi held the first of what were to become regular weekly meetings. After considering the Middle East crisis their attention was turned to the scene at home. According to Egyptian press reports Dr Fawzi asked the President what he believed most interested the citizens. President Sadat replied that the people wished to feel that matters concerning them were being taken seriously and that the government was conscious of their problems and was dealing with them capably. The Prime Minister agreed and said he was taking into consideration the basic rule that the masses of the people came before anything else and that government must during the coming stage form a relationship of trust with the masses. A heady conversation, but it did indicate that in spite of numerous and regular public statements about the Middle East crisis, the problems of the Egyptian people were also being considered.

At a press conference two days later Mr Kamal Henry Badir, the Minister of Communications, announced that 100,000 new telephone lines would be installed during the fiscal year to alleviate the internal communications problem.

On the last day of October the Cabinet, meeting under the chairmanship of President Sadat, decided to cut the prices of some essential consumer goods. The goods affected were tea, sugar, kerosene, radio sets, refrigerators, electric batteries, shoes and pullovers.

The government also decided to promote 150,000 government sector employees who were overdue for promotion. They approved the advancing of the payment of the personal shares in profits of the public sector to the employees.

Of course the idea of the price cuts was not merely benevolence; the government was hoping the cuts would induce spending by the masses in turn helping the desperately shaky economy. National Guidance Minister Mohammed Fayek pointed out following the meeting: "It is a step on the path of consolidating our economy. Our economic support is real support for our armed forces."

But perhaps more important than the obvious needs of the people, the government was also concentrating on the less obvious - or so it would appear from a report in the weekly *Akhbar el Yom*. The article dealt with Colonel Aly Helmy, the chief of the police's criminal investigation department in Cairo who was "resolved to wipe out the phenomenon of pick-pocketing in the capital." It said: "Thirteen gangs of pickpockets were rounded up recently. The purging process is going on and every morning a police lorry returns with scores of pickpockets, suspects, swindlers, forgers and law evaders, and a big assortment of pens, glasses, wrist watches, empty wallets and identity cards."

Therefore within a month of President Sadat coming into office several community services had been commenced if not completed. However in Egypt with its rapidly growing population and continual need for housing, food and plain capital to enable investment, there was always plenty to occupy the minds of an aware government.

Politically, probably the more important domestic policy of the new government was the decision to carry out widespread de-sequestration of property.

The first sequestration order of the post 1952 Revolution government had been a decree law issued in 1952 imposing sequestration on the property and funds of

King Farouk. This was followed a few years later by the nationalisation of the Suez Canal Company.

However the major batch of foreign sequestrations took place following the 1956 Suez Crisis. This was not entirely surprising as a considerable amount of foreign investment at the time was French and British. The part played by the French and British in the crisis laid the foreign businesses open for revenge by the angry Egyptian government.

The major sequestrations involving Egyptians did not take place until between October 1961 and February 1962. In the five-month period 600 of Egypt's wealthiest families had their property sequestrated by the state. Many of these families were Copts or Jews which led to the accusation that the measures were based on religious discrimination. But although there may be some truth in this, the government was always able to argue that within the top bracket of Egyptian income earners were considerable numbers of both Copts and Jews.

Sequestration had taken place from time to time, although not on the same scale, up until the time President Sadat decided to liquidate sequestration late in December 1970 - just over two months after taking office. The presidential decree was considered a practical realisation of demands calling for the codification of the revolution and the sovereignty of law.

Sadat asked the Prime Minister to arrange the liquidation of existing sequestration through legal committees. Also to present to the National Assembly legislation whereby the imposition of sequestration in the future would be governed by legal controls providing the protection of the people's socialist gains and national security. Any further sequestration measures would be taken with guarantees protecting the individual within the framework of the protection of the society. It was decided that sequestration in the future would only be in accordance with legislation and by a special court including, beside special judges assigned to the task of applying the provisions of the law, individuals on the lines of a jury to ensure the people's participation and control. Therefore under Sadat's plan no more indiscriminate state sequestration could take place, but instead it would become a matter of a judicial nature protecting the rights of the people.

When President Sadat made the decision there were some 140 families whose property and funds were under security sequestration in addition to some 10,000 outstanding accounts pertaining to former cases of property and funds under sequestration.

A timetable was set for the settling of these cases and accounts taking into account taxes due on them and incomes of agricultural land involved. The timetable provided for complete liquidation by the end of 1971.

De-sequestration had taken place from time to time much before President Sadat's decision, however, and it was reported at the time that 90 per cent of cases of sequestration imposed following the 1956 Suez Crisis had already been liquidated.

President Sadat's de-sequestration decree was welcomed warmly by Egyptian businessmen and economists who said it would ensure stability for citizens who were wary of investing their private funds. The action would open the way for investment by the private sector. As well as being a socially correct thing to do it was to provide the economy, struggling from lack of investment, a much-needed boost.

The majority of decisions involving the masses during the first months of the government headed by Dr Fawzi and Sadat were aimed, at least in part, at stimulating the economy which had been stultified ever since foreign investment subsided in the early post-revolution years. The idea was in fact to bring consumer goods into the reach of more people thus creating a demand for more goods. By providing security against sequestration the government was inducing Egyptian investors to put their savings into Egyptian industries and commercial ventures. The fact was that although de-sequestration had obviously had a considerable effect and had greatly reduced the number of extremely rich Egyptians who prior to the Revolution in 1952 would pass their nights in the many casinos and night clubs in both Cairo and Alexandria, there were still a considerable number of people in the millionaire class living in Egypt. Many of these people were merely sitting on their fortunes not wishing to risk the uncertainty of Egyptian commerce. The important thing for a greater part of the consumer market industries sector was not to get money from outside Egypt, but to induce Egyptians with money to reinvest in Egypt.

Early in February 1971 the government took another step in the direction of inducing the people as a whole to spend more to stimulate the consumer economy by making a conscious effort to reduce the cost of living. In fact one English news broadcast on Radio Cairo stated quite categorically that from such and such a date the cost of living would be reduced.

11. A shoeshiner's windfall in Luxor. Russian aid to Egypt

Luxor was just the place to spend the winter. A winter's paradise, it was. Always it had been a place to escape to away from Cairo's cold winter. The rich had always migrated there having spent the summer in Alexandria with its golden beaches and exotic night clubs and casinos, although these had become tarnished since the revolution without the patronage of the monarch. Still, a lot of people continued the routine. American tourists had replaced the British and French and took Luxor in as part of their whirlwind tours. A lot of Russians also visited Luxor and they wore shoes like everyone else although as far as Hassan was concerned they did not drop piasters like the Americans. But they still liked to have their shoes shined. They were not mean though. Better to clean the shoes of a Russian than an Egyptian, thought Hassan. But many of them did not speak English which was a disadvantage, and even fewer spoke Arabic. But then, the shine was the main thing. One did not have to talk to make shoes shine. Although it made things more interesting.

How beautiful the winter was in Luxor. If Hassan had been in Cairo he would have been continually shivering with his head wrapped up in rugs to drive the influenza away. And sickness cost money - not in medicines, but in time lost when shoes could not be shined. It was really a wonder more people did not come to Luxor for the winter. A real wonder, Hassan thought.

Standing out in front of the Luxor Hotel overlooking the Luxor Temple was a pleasure in itself. Hardly noticed the shining. With the sun - a nice warm sun, not an unpleasant sun like in summer - on your back, it was a pleasure to get to work each day. A pleasure indeed, it was. The temple was magnificent standing there for all those years baking in the continual sunshine. How beautiful it must have been in days gone past when it was complete. Hassan often stood just looking at its splendour with the sun catching the sand-coloured stone of which it was built.

In those days I wonder if there were shoeshiners, thought Hassan. Then he was cut short.

"A shine please," came a voice. A shine please: here was someone actually asking for a shine? Here was a man asking for a shine without being badgered and annoyed until he finally relented and agreed to have his shoes shined? Life in Luxor was really something extraordinary for Hassan. What is more he looked rich: worth at least fifteen piasters.

"Speak English?" enquired Hassan as he got down on his knees to commence the job.

"Yes," uttered the man dumbfounded by the irony of this Egyptian shoeshine man asking him whether he spoke English. "Do you?"

"Of course friend," said Hassan.

Of course questioned the man in his mind? Of course? Where does an Egyptian shoeshiner learn to speak English so well? The man put his thoughts into words: "Where did you learn English?"

"I worked for a man from England who drank a bottle of whisky every night."

"A bottle of whisky every day?" questioned the man.

"Yes a bottle of whisky every day. Too much, eh," said Hassan going through the same old story with obvious relish.

"Too much, yes," agreed the man.

"Why? Don't you like whisky?"

"Yes," replied the man, "but not a bottle a day."

"No?" A smile followed Hassan's question.

"No. Do you like whisky?"

"Me? Shoeshiners don't drink whisky in Egypt."

"Don't they," commented the man.

"No. Do they where you come from? Where do you come from friend?"

"Canada."

"Ah Canada, I thought America from your voice."

"Do shoeshiners drink whisky in Canada?"

The man dodged the question not really knowing any shoeshiners in Canada and knowing still less whether they drank whisky or not. "I clean my own shoes at home."

"Clean you own shoes?"

"Yes."

Hassan thought that was pretty mean. Here was a man who was so mean that he usually cleaned his own shoes. "Why don't you clean your own shoes when you are in Egypt?"

"I don't have any polish."

"Why don't you buy polish?"

"I thought I would let you shine them. I thought you would make them cleaner."

"That is good," said Hassan. "I will make them much cleaner than you could, my friend." He unscrewed a tin of grease and rubbed a finger around the rim and then fingered it into the shoes. "This . . . this will make them like new."

The shoes finished the man handed Hassan ten piasters. "Thank you," said Hassan.

The man walked off away from the hotel down the street towards the entrance of the Luxor Temple. Hassan, seeing no reason why the conversation should come to a stop just because the man's shoes were shined, followed. The man one step ahead, the two rounded the corner and continued along the footpath of the corniche. After about fifty yards the man stopped, slightly bewildered by Hassan following. "I paid you didn't I?" questioned the man.

"Yes," said Hassan.

The man continued walking and Hassan continued following. "Why are you following me?"

"Have you a guide?"

"No."

"Do you need a guide?"

"I don't think so."

"Better to have a guide otherwise you will pay people a lot of piasters for doing nothing and you will not know what anything is anyway."

"Really?" Perhaps he is right, thought the man, and he does speak English. He might be a help.

"How much for the morning?"

"I will take you to Luxor Temple then across the river to the monuments at Thebes and you get back to your hotel about half past two just in time for lunch. Sound good?"

"Piasters, how much?"

"As you like friend," said Hassan.

"No how much?"

"One pound the whole time."

"Seventy five piasters," bargained the man.

"Yes, seventy five piasters for you friend."

The two arrived at the ticket office. The man had a ticket for all the monuments so he did not have to pay and Hassan did not have to pay because he knew the ticket man. Hassan negotiated with the ticket man to look after his shine box for one shine later in the day because he was changing profession for a day. Then he led the man around the temple pointing out as much as he knew and a lot that he didn't know. The man was impressed but probably more by the temple than the description by Hassan.

Up walked a man in a galabia with a scarf around his head. This man started to explain a frieze around the top of one of the columns but was cut short by Hassan. "This man he doesn't need a guide," Hassan told the man in English although they both spoke Arabic naturally. It was to impress the man who was being saved piasters here and there.

The Luxor Temple having been covered adequately Hassan led the man along the corniche towards the jetty of a ferry which crossed the river. "Luxor Temple good?"

"Yes, very good thank you," said the man.

"I will now take you across the river to Thebes where there are a lot of other temples and tombs in the ground. They are very good you will like them."

"Thank you."

"I think we should hire bicycles to tour Thebes on or would you like a taxi? Perhaps a taxi would be better? Or would you like to ride a donkey? But a donkey is too slow you will not see very much if you ride a donkey. Either bicycle or taxi would be best. Yes a taxi would be best."

"No I think bicycles would be best. It would give me a bit of much-needed exercise."

"As you wish," said Hassan.

The two negotiated with a man to hire two bicycles for the morning. It cost them forty piasters each bicycle. During the negotiations Hassan periodically butted in with a few sentences in Arabic to give the man the impression he was getting the best possible deal.

"Lucky you have me. Lucky I speak Arabic. That man charge you fifty piasters otherwise," said Hassan taking no account of the fact that the man had had to hire two bicycles instead of one because he was with him.

"Yes, thank you," said the man.

"Now I will save you more piasters. Instead of crossing the river Nile on the tourist boat we will go on the smaller boat that takes the people. Only a piaster each way each - that is good isn't it?"

The man agreed and the two rode their bikes to the top of the river embankment near where the small boat left from, hopped off and pushed them down the bank. Then they lifted the bikes on to the boat which was already at the jetty waiting. They took seats in the sun near the bow. Other people were carrying on bags of onions, potatoes and other produce which was on its way across to the small village on the other side of the river. A small boy selling peanuts came up to the man and offered him some.

"Like peanuts?" Hassan questioned the man.

"Yes, but no thank you."

"They are very good. They are the best in Egypt. Egyptian peanuts very good, friend."

"Alright." The man took five piasters worth and they settled down for the short voyage. When they crossed the river another passenger insisted on carrying the man's bicycle off the boat and on to the shore. "But I can carry it myself," protested the man. He knew he was expected to pay a couple of piasters for the task.

"Does the man want baksheesh?" the man asked Hassan.

"Not baksheesh," said Hassan indignantly. "He has done something to earn the money. That is not baksheesh. Baksheesh if he does nothing for the money. Give him two piasters."

The man with Hassan was thanked and the words were uttered: "Welcome to our country."

"Thank you," said the man sarcastically. "Thank you a lot."

The surface on the path was not smooth so they had to push the bikes about two hundred yards across a swampy bit of land until they got to the surfaced road. Then they hopped on the bicycles and started riding down the tarred road towards the Valley of the Queens. Their first stop was at two giant statues built by Amenhotep III. They stood in the midst of a sugar cane field beside the road. An old man was squatting on the side of the road beside a straw mat on which were arranged brooches made of local stone and filigree jewellery. As he saw the two arriving he said: "Like to have a look? Good morning."

Hassan and the man had hopped off their bikes by this stage, but just walked past the man hardly giving a look.

"Like to just have a look. No charge for lookin," said the old man in vain.

Having had a quick look at the colossi the two rode off again, Hassan keeping the tail of his galabia in his mouth to keep it away from the chain. Once he remembered he had been riding happily across the fields and suddenly his galabia had got caught in the chain. It had taken him several hours to get himself unknotted again. But never again, he was making sure of that, by the Prophet.

The morning passed and the two got quite hot riding along without any protection from the midday sun. From one monument to another, they went, until they had completed the tour. Then they retraced their steps and caught the boat back across the river paying the one piaster for the trip again.

Past the Luxor Temple picking up Hassan's shining box on the way and back to the Luxor Hotel, they went. At the entrance of the hotel they halted for the transaction of business to take place formally.

"Seventy five piasters, you said."

"As you like," Hassan said rather half heartedly. "As you like."

"You said seventy five piasters so here are seventy five piasters," said the man handing Hassan the money. Hassan's hand remained outstretched as if he had not registered that he had already been paid. The man dug into his pocket and lifted out another ten piasters and handed it to Hassan.

"Thank you my friend," said Hassan.

"Thank you indeed," said the man.

Then as if as an afterthought Hassan said: "Your shoes need a shine. Like a shine?"

The man looked down. Sure enough the shoes were caked in desert dust. He reluctantly said yes. Another ten piasters was handed to Hassan.

It had been a special day for Hassan. A day in a million earning all those piasters, thought Hassan. As a final farewell to the man he uttered: "Welcome to our country." The man just waved as he disappeared into the hotel.

***

"Our friendship with the Soviet Union is not merely to side with it, but to side with independence, nationalism, and social and political freedom. Our friendship with the Soviet Union is at the same time a stand of solidarity embracing all the anti-imperialistic powers. The Soviet Union's friendly stand towards us and aversion to Israel's expansionist aggressive ambitions and its terrorist role on this land, is nothing but a stand against imperialism and its instruments. I have, brothers, to record here and to comment on the sincere, honest aid which the Soviet Union has extended and is extending to us, and its unselfish support for us in times of ordeals and hardships as an assured friend on the one hand, and as a major power in the world on the other. The Soviet Union has sought to establish peace based on justice and to have the law of justice prevail in the world, instead of the law of the jungle and aggression."

The words were those of President Sadat. He was addressing the country's National Assembly on November 19, 1970, just over a month after coming into office. Hardly a speech, if any at all, that Sadat made during his first six months as president neglected to mention the aid that the Soviet Union had given Egypt, both military and civil.

Egypt genuinely had a lot to be grateful to the Soviet Union for providing. They were just completing the High Dam, they had rebuilt the armed forces since the seemingly ruinous defeat in 1967 in the Six Day War, they were pouring money and experts into land reclamation schemes, building dockyards and giving valuable support to the United Arab Republic diplomatically, directly with the United States, through the United Nations and through the Big Four.

Just how much they were asking in return is uncertain but it can be assumed that Russia at least approved the appointment of Sadat and Fawzi although neither were hard core socialists and were definitely not communists. They believed in the rights of the people and the good of the country and in whatever political system could achieve this end. They were in fact extremely idealistic like the creators of the revolution - Sadat having been one himself. The Russians would have also approved the cabinet.

It was of course in Russia's interest to help Egypt and the Arabs even if it were only to get access to Egypt's Mediterranean-side ports, these ports being what Russia needed most. But while Russia had a lot to gain from helping Egypt and Egypt had a lot to gain by accepting help, the Russians knew all too well that they did not have anything like the relationship with Cairo that they had with Prague or Budapest. Although Cairo had been knocked back in the past by the West for aid and obviously it was easier to get aid from Moscow, it would not be impossible for her to get arms from elsewhere. Of course not on the terms that Russia gave, but she could get them all the same.

The Russians were conscious of the fact also that the Egyptian class above the ordinary fellahin was more impressed with the American way of life than the Russian counterpart and the most popular consumer goods were those made under licence and which in Arabic and English had on their packets: "America's favourite". The Egyptian community, through no fault or dislike of the Russians but rather due to their heritage and upbringing with British and French influence was fairly materialistic although earning very little. Although there were a growing number of Russian-built cars on Egypt's roads, for instance, the majority were still West European, the British having fallen off due to embargoes on cars made by companies which also had plants in Israel.

The Russians, about 20,000 at the beginning of 1971, tended to live fairly much with themselves. However they were really not unpopular as some reports indicated.

During the funeral week of Nasser, Sadat, who was then interim president, had several meetings with Soviet Premier Kosygin who had flown to Cairo. How much they actually discussed about government after Nasser is uncertain, but the meetings did form the basis of closer and closer ties with Russia which showed themselves in increased military aid for Egypt. The ceasefire was in force and it was the determination of Kosygin and Sadat to make the most of the standstill to bolster the armed forces. Intelligence reports indicated that an incredible amount of new equipment was shipped to Egypt during the first six months of the ceasefire through Alexandria and assembled both along the Suez Canal and in other strategic positions.

Egypt, after Nasser as before his death, was continually being visited by distinguished Soviets from President

Nikolai Podgorny down. Following Kosygin's visit there were visits by film stars and technicians, the Kiev Ballet, three Cosmonauts (at the time of the Apollo 14 trip to the moon incidentally, whether or not that was of any significance), hundreds of tourists, all with the avowed intention of meeting their friends the Egyptians and letting the Egyptians see that they were human as well as efficiently generous.

The Russian involvement in Egypt which had steadily increased since the 1956 Suez crisis and the rejection of aid by the United States for Egypt's High Dam project, reached a pinnacle during the early ceasefire period which started in August 1970. This provided an obvious opportunity to build up as well as train an army which previously had been fighting Nasser's War of Attrition. A month after the ceasefire came into force Nasser died, placing a great need on the Egyptian government to prove that a vacuum had not developed due to the lack of the dynamic leader. Obviously it was in Russia's interests to make sure of this also so they continued to build up Egypt's armaments and committed themselves to more and more social projects.

Russia may not have been perturbed by the transition of power to Sadat, lesser known and obviously politically weaker than Nasser. It perhaps gave them an opportunity to control more and have more part in the running of the country.

The influence of Russia during the first months of Sadat's employ, it seemed, was moderating, encouraging diplomacy rather than war as a means of retrieving the lands lost in 1967. However confident Russia might have been as regards Egypt's military capability they must also have known that as with all battles there was a risk. A risk, moreover, too doubtful to take. If Egypt had again been defeated it would have been a very bad blow to the prestige of the Soviet Union. Egypt was too obviously supported by Russia and Israel too obviously supported by the United States. It would have been a bad advertisement for Russian arms. Another point of course was that Russia more than anybody else would benefit from the re-opening of the Suez Canal. Anyone with a map showing the proximity of Russia's Black Sea ports with the Red Sea by way of the canal would agree. If war broke out and should Israel at least maintain her then post-1967 borders, it would stabilize and freeze the situation for several years until diplomacy reached this stage again.

Russia was included in the first batch of countries to be visited by special envoys of Sadat in Egypt's mammoth diplomatic campaign following the passing of the Afro-Asian resolution at the United Nations. Presumably not because Egypt had to persuade her benevolent friend to support her cause as she did in some other world capitals, but to secure and guarantee more arms. If the United States was supplying Israel with arms to put her into a strong bargaining position for the resumed Jarring contacts, Russia was required to do the same for Egypt. Russia had to balance power. As part of this Russia increased the supply of offensive weapons including tanks, mobile bridges and artillery as well as maintaining the flow of missiles for the air defence system. Prior to the ceasefire the majority of arms supplied to Egypt had been defensive, but offensive weapon supply was increasing. Obviously a country which wanted a diplomatic solution, but which was continually stating that it was prepared to take other remedies to retrieve its lost land was not going to be taken seriously if equipped only with mainly defensive weapons.

It was in such a climate that Vice President Aly Sabry led his delegation to Moscow as part of the diplomatic drive. When this delegation's visit to Moscow was announced in Cairo it was said that although it would have several assignments it would seize the opportunity of expounding in detail Egypt's viewpoint on the developments which had taken place since the last meeting held between Sadat and Kosygin. That had been at the time of Nasser's funeral.

On December 21, 1970 the talks began in Moscow. As an indication of the importance of the talks the Soviet delegation was led by none less than Leonid Brezhnev, secretary of the Soviet Communist Party Central Committee, President Nikolai Podgorny and Premier Alexei Kosygin. The Egyptian side, led by Vice President Aly Sabry, also comprised Dr Aziz Sidky, Deputy Premier and Minister of Education, Mr Riad, Deputy Premier and Foreign Minister, and General Mohammed Fawzy, the War Minister.

An official said following the first round of talks that they dealt with bilateral relations, the Middle East crisis and the stand of the Big Four and the developments of the Jarring Mission. However unofficially observers believed that even at this first meeting between the two sides Russia declared that she was ready to increase the military and economic aid to Egypt. In a banquet address that evening Mr Kosygin guaranteed a steady flow of weapons, financial aid and know-how to the United Arab Republic.

Turning to the Middle East crisis generally, he said: "As a result of aggression by Israel supported by the United States, the Middle East has been made one of the most dangerous breeding grounds of war danger in the world. Here the forces of national liberation and progress are confronting the forces of imperialistic aggression, giving them an even stronger rebuff." He went on to say that Russia welcomed the stand of Egypt aimed at strengthening the unity of Arab countries and mobilising all their potentials in the struggle for elimination of the Israeli aggression.

Vice President Sabry said in reply that Egypt's relations with Russia were not something transient. They were strong and developing relations based on the common struggle for liberation and progress. "We see that the United States is giving constant and open aid to Israel thus encouraging the Israeli aggression against the Arab states and helping to consolidate Zionist expansion at the expense of the Arab peoples. We see that the close American-Israeli alliance is directed against the Arab peoples, against their future, against their interests," said the Vice President.

Later he stressed Russia's generosity. "Our people in the United Arab Republic and throughout the vast Arab homeland will never forget the resolute and noble stand of the Soviet Union which is on our side in the just and decisive struggle waged by the Arab people against the Israeli aggressors and against the forces of world imperialism."

In a joint communiqué released at the conclusion of the talks, Russia declared that it would continue to extend aid and support for the Arab people in their struggle for the liberation of their occupied land and the establishment of a just peace in the Middle East. The communiqué expressed the countries' full faith that a "just and lasting" peace in the Middle East could only be achieved through the full implementation of the Security Council Resolution of November 1967, the withdrawal of the Israeli forces from all occupied Arab territories, and the execution of the United Nations' resolutions confirming the legitimate rights of the Palestinian people.

Commenting editorially on the communiqué, *Al Ahram* said: "It will have its far-reaching repercussions on confronting Israel's attempts to obstruct every solution for the Middle East crisis and to freeze the situation. These attempts of Israel are backed by the forces of world imperialism led by the United States. The communiqué is certainly a further step in consolidating the close and friendly relations between the U.A.R. and the Soviet Union. It stresses the unity of action and integration among all anti-imperialistic forces for peace, national independence, social progress, democracy and socialism."

Although increased aid both civil and military was forthcoming following this meeting in Moscow, it was not until the middle of January when President Podgorny was in Egypt for the formal celebrations marking the completion of the Russian-built High Dam that any specific item apart from broad generalisations was announced. President Podgorny, at a mass rally in Aswan following the ceremonies at the dam site announced that the Soviet Union would assist Egypt in completing electrification of all Egyptian villages. He also announced furthering of projects of land reclamation. The electrification scheme was believed to be of more than the obvious importance. It was thought that the bringing of electric light to small, out of the way villages would have an effect on reducing the birth rate by reducing the boredom of the night hours.

Therefore Russia had been associated with the three most important schemes in Egyptian eyes since the 1952 revolution. They were namely, the High Dam, the rehabilitation of the armed forces and the electrification scheme. There were also several other schemes such as land reclamation and the building of the Alexandria dockyard which should not be forgotten.

Had it not been for one decision, however, all could have been different. Had the United States rather than the Soviet Union built the dam, the whole recent history of the Middle East might be different. Britain and the U.S. had agreed to grant $70 million to finance the dam and the World Bank had agreed to supply a further $200 million. But following Nasser's decision to buy arms from Czechoslovakia and Egypt's recognition of Communist China in May 1956, plus a generally deteriorating relationship between Egypt and the West, the finance was withdrawn. It was not long before Russia took the West's place and agreed to finance the dam, but evidently not without some hesitation. In 1956 Mr Daniel Solod, Soviet Ambassador in Cairo, evidently was heard to remark that Russia was not sure whether it wanted to finance the project. But he observed that if the West built it Egypt would be Western-oriented for twenty years. In the event Russia built the dam.

The ceremonies in Aswan underlined the validity of the Soviet ambassador's remarks. Sadat, who commended the Soviet aid, contrasted it with the stand adopted by the United States. He referred to America's offer to finance the High Dam and said that America had broken her promise. He went on to say that this broken American promise was neither the first nor the last broken by those who had given it.

Then he documented the broken promises. In 1953 they had promised to supply Egypt with arms, but they had broken this promise and supplied arms to Israel. In

1956 they promised to assist in building the dam, but withdrew the loans. In 1967 they gave a promise to preserve the territorial integrity of the countries of the Middle East, but supported Israeli aggression. In 1968 they gave Egypt the promise to assist in the implementation of the United Nations' Security Council Resolution, but the same year gave Phantom aircraft to Israel. In 1969 they affirmed the necessity of solving the crisis, but continued to support Israel. In 1970 when the Rogers (Secretary of State) peace initiative was launched they gave Israel $500 million of aid.

Sadat added: "Every broken and unfulfilled promise on the part of America is countered by a Soviet promise which has been fulfilled or is on its way to fulfilment."

So Russia was in Egypt. But what did the military involvement entail? Repeatedly Sadat said that reports that Russians manned the missile system and other military appliances were devoid of truth. "These bases are manned by Egyptians and we do not want others to fight our battle" was a favourite phrase of the president. However American and British intelligence reports would indicate otherwise.

It seems that the Russians did man the SAM 3 missile system and to a lesser extent, the less sophisticated SAM 2 system. On both models Russian advisors would be instructing the Egyptians on their use, but there was no real indication and in fact early in 1971 it seemed incomprehensible that the students could have graduated to full control of the SAM 3. In the Navy and Air Force there were many Soviet advisors, but those in the Navy had orders to leave the ships when any trouble occurred, if possible.

The Israelis claimed Russians did fly sorties before the ceasefire came into effect. But the Egyptians denied this.

Despite Sadat's harsh statements about America there were indications that he would have greatly welcomed an improved relationship with the United States, a fact which must have worried Russia. It is this which also prompted Russia to continue committing aid to Egypt. Had aid lagged following the completion of the High Dam, Egypt could have said thank you for your help and goodbye. This was highly unlikely, but it would have been possible. All Russians would have had to leave and ten years of work would have been wasted. But with the electrification project and others this was unthinkable.

As I mentioned briefly, all was not one-sided. Egypt was providing Russia with water and some provisions for her Navy vessels which used the port of Alexandria. Evidently when Russian vessels used the new Russian-built Alexandria dockyard, they paid for their berths. But this was not as harsh as it might seem as the payment was a way of reducing the giant loans extended to Egypt by Russia. Russia paid for the berths by subtracting the amount from the loans outstanding.

12. The Aswan High Dam

When Soviet President Nikolai Podgorny stood with President Sadat atop the huge High Dam on January 15, 1971 he was more than inaugurating the completion of a giant project. He was placing the Hammer and Sickle seal firmly on what to the Egyptians was undoubtedly the greatest single achievement of the post-revolution era. It was Nasser's dream come true. It was a project planned to have an effect on almost every facet of the Egyptian economy from providing much needed electric power to preventing the flooding Nile from spoiling crops and inundating villages.

The work on the dam was officially started on January 9 1960, when excavation of a diversion canal for the Nile began. Three years later President Nasser threw the first granite stone into the river marking the start of work on the building of the rock-fill dam. In May the following year, 1964, the dam had reached such a stage that the river was diverted into the canal. In 1968 the first three power units in the hydro-electric plants were commissioned sending power along the cables to Cairo. On the eighteenth anniversary of the 1952 Revolution, celebrations took place in Aswan marking the completion of the last of the twelve electric generators.

The project became to Nasser a symbol of the benefits to Egypt of the revolution he had engineered. It became an emotional obsession. So much so that it became sacrilege to question the validity of spending so much finance on one project. So much so that any criticism of it became a personal slight on Nasser himself.

In 1960 Dr Abdel Aziz Ahmed, an Egyptian hydrologist, addressing a gathering of civil engineers in London, warned of the consequences of building the High Dam. He said it would cause agricultural and ecological problems and would be an unwise project. When Dr Ahmed returned to Cairo he was retired.

Nasser had fought hard to finance the dam. American-spearheaded Western loans withdrawn, he nationalised the Suez Canal Company in theory to help finance the dam, but also out of anger at the West. This nationalisation caused the 1956 Suez crisis thus stoking more emotion on the High Dam fire. But as we know the Russians agreed to help, and Egypt got the dam.

Due to the emotion surrounding the project even in 1970 only good things about the dam were said publicly in Egypt, although unofficially it was causing a number of headaches. Because few people had reason to doubt what Egypt was saying about their mighty dam, or perhaps because of lack of interest, the world had also tended to hear only of the advantages of the project. But about the time of the opening ceremonies in January, 1971, many exposés on the dam were published throughout the world. Some were more frightening than others and some led one to believe that the project had been a complete failure.

True, there had always been problems associated with the dam, some were predicted before the dam was completed; others were not. But the Egyptians would still insist that the project was worthwhile. Long before the time of Nasser the dam was dreamed of as a long-term solution to the problem of flooding and in fact as a way of harnessing the water which flooded wasted into the sea.

But it was to be a long-term solution. Although there were many problems the advantages over the decades could be expected to make it worthwhile. Two hundred years seemed little to a civilization already over four thousand years old.

One of the greatest reasons for disappointment was that the Egyptians always placed too much emphasis on what the dam would give them, but perhaps this was not surprising with a project costing more than $1,000 million.

Apart from restraining the sometimes ruinous flood waters and producing enough hydro-electricity for Egypt, the 364-foot high dam situated about ten miles upstream from Aswan, was to increase agricultural output through more efficient irrigation and the reclamation of land, stimulate industry using the cheap hydro-power, create a giant fishing industry in Lake Nasser behind the dam, and generally make Egypt's economy more predictable. In short it was going to boost Egypt's national income and pay for itself in two years.

In reality it restrained flood waters, but with disadvantages. Once the floods carried from the river's mountainous source in the heart of Africa volcanic sediment which continually rejuvenated the valley and made it one of the natural agricultural wonders of the world. Now without the sediment-filled flood waters the land was becoming impoverished and thousands of pounds were being spent on fertilisers which were not previously needed. The floods, although causing much loss of life, also carried away with them soil salts and snails carrying the bilharzia germ. Now salts were accumulating and bilharzia was spreading. To combat both of these the Egyptian government was spending considerable funds.

In reality the hydro-electric generators were capable in 1971 of producing almost three times as much power as Egypt could consume leaving ten of the twelve generators virtually unused. This might change with the proposed expansion of industry, but this expansion was not taking place and was unlikely to because of lack of capital.

In reality land was being reclaimed, but not at the rate predicted. And the cost was to some making the value of the reclamation questionable.

In reality there were plenty of fish in Lake Nasser, but due to the harshness of the terrain surrounding the lake and the almost intolerable heat much of the year, they were not being fished to capacity. Further downstream and in the Mediterranean near the mouth of the river, fishing suffered due to less plankton being supplied to the marine life, now that the dam retained the silt at Aswan.

The dam and the build-up of the giant Lake Nasser forced the resettlement of some 50,000 Nubians in newly reclaimed areas. Although there were cases of dissatisfaction many were happily resettled in an area of some 38,000 acres. Houses were built and other social services provided. Nubian temples which were in any case flooded every year were transferred and re-erected well above the water level of the new lake.

The importance of the High Dam made the government very conscious of the need for adequate protection. Although the rock-fill dam could not be destroyed itself with anything short of an atomic weapon, its hydro-electric plant and ancillary services could be destroyed with conventional weapons. Early in 1971 it was believed that it was defended by three SAM 3 missile sites and several airfields established both close to the dam and along the Red Sea coast. Standing on the crest of the dam one could see on the distant desert horizon, the radar system of a missile going around and around scanning the skies for enemy aircraft.

On the day of the completion ceremonies there was a placard atop the dam which read: "The High Dam finished, now for Palestine." Some journalist suggested facetiously that perhaps the Russians were now going to help the Arabs built a dam across the Jordan River to flood the Israelis out of Palestine.

13. Tragedy in Abu el Feda. Government moves on Education

Dokki's pregnant wife had awakened with terrible pains. A doctor had to be called. She had been taken away to a hospital and put in a ward with nineteen other women - all pregnant. But she was only four months pregnant. The other women were all due to give birth to their babies. She lay in agony.

Dokki returned to Abu el Feda after sitting with his wife for the morning. In silence he sat beside her. He was to go back in the evening to see her again following the doctor's inspection. In Abu el Feda he stood staring into space. He just thought as the hours passed slowly. The bustle of the day passed in front of his glazed eyes. He acknowledged the greetings, but unknowingly.

Sabra was carrying on the duties which had to be done. She was delivering beer and charcoal to residents who had ordered them. She nursed her smallest brother. She played with her other brother and sister. Her day passed busily.

Hakki was carrying on his pushing and moving of cars in the garage. It was just a normal day in many respects, but not for Dokki. He was thinking of his wife. Why did he deserve this, he wondered? Whatever the reason it was happening and that was all there was about it. No use wondering why, but he could not help it.

Along the road came Mahmoud pedalling his tricycle. His greeting to Dokki fell at first upon deaf ears. But he persisted. "Sa'id Dokki."

Dokki shook his head as he heard Mahmoud's voice. "Sa'id my friend."

"By the Prophet I thought you were asleep."

"Ah yes my friend," said Dokki forcing a smile.

"By the Prophet what is wrong?"

"It is my wife."

"Your wife?"

"Yes."

Hakki walked closer, not joining in the conversation, but just listening. He had heard he whole thing earlier but it is not often something more exciting than a cloud of rain bursts on Abu el Feda. This in spite of its tragedy was a respite from the boredom.

"What is the matter with your wife, Dokki?"

"She is very sick and she is in hospital."

"That is no good. That is no good." Mahmoud stood by his tricycle shaking his head in pity. Hakki looked at Mahmoud and then at Dokki to see who was going to utter the next words.

"Early this morning she woke with very bad pains."

"That is no good," said Mahmoud.

"I went round the corner to the pharmacy, but he said I should take her to hospital."

"That is no good."

"By the Prophet it was no good."

The head shaking continued without a word being uttered. Hakki drifted back to the garage to continue polishing a car.

The minutes passing Mahmoud lifted a gas container from his tricycle and threw it on to his shoulder. Then he walked up the front steps of the flats and inside. When he returned with the empty cylinder, Dokki was still just standing, thinking.

"By the Prophet, Dokki, you had better not worry too much. All will be well."

"That is right," said Dokki, "All will be well I hope."

Mahmoud placed the cylinder on to the tricycle and sat on the seat. As he placed all his weight on one pedal the tricycle slowly started to move.

"Farewell. All will be well."

"By the Prophet thank you Mahmoud."

"I will see you later today," said Mahmoud.

"God willing . . . Inshalah."

A man came along after some time swinging a shoeshine box. He asked Dokki if he would like his shoes shined. Dokki agreed. He put his foot upon the rest and the man started shining. They talked about nothing in particular. Dokki did not know the man so the conversation did not arise regarding his wife for some time. But eventually it did. Things are that way among the Egyptian people. Nothing is secret. Nothing is hidden from anyone who enquired. Everyone is everybody's friend much of the time.

"That is no good," said the man being told about Dokki's wife. "No good."

Night began to fall so Dokki prepared himself and began his walk to the hospital. He made his way along the Cairo streets in a daze not thinking of anything else but what he would hear when he arrived at the hospital. By the Prophet all is well, he hoped.

He arrived at the drab hospital just as the street lights were turned on signalling the end of another day and the beginning of another night. It was a converted mansion on Zamalek and the entrance was dark and dreary. Dokki was shown into a small room where the paint was peeling from the walls and a few old newspapers lay on the table.

"But can I not see my wife?" asked Dokki.

"Soon enough," came the reply.

So Dokki resigned himself to waiting for the Egyptian bureaucracy which had even affected the treating of human beings, to catch up on itself. Or not to catch up with itself because that was an impossibility in a country with thirty-four million people and a great shortage of doctors, but at least to catch up enough to let him see his wife. That was all he cared about. He was given a number and when that was called he could go to the ward where his wife was in bed. His number was 104, but he presumed there were not 103 people waiting.

He sat down in the room with ten other people. They all sat quietly. One man had a handful of peanuts, and was eating them, but the others just sat looking into space.

After about ten minutes a nurse came and beckoned to Dokki. Dokki followed her out of the room. She said the news was good and bad.

"Good and bad, by the Prophet what do you mean?" questioned Dokki.

"Your wife is alright but there will be no baby."

"No baby? But why?"

The nurse went into a long explanation which Dokki did not understand.

"But you said my wife is going to be alright?"

"Yes."

"That is good by the Prophet."

He was then led into the room where his wife was lying. They talked for a while then his wife fell asleep. He quietly left for home. The end of an eventful day. He slept soundly.

By the Prophet it was a better day when Dokki woke. Nothing to worry about now. Mahmoud was one of the earliest passers-by.

"By the Prophet that is good," said Mahmoud in response to Dokki's statement that his wife was to be alright. "That is very good."

"Very good indeed by the Prophet," said Dokki.

Hakki walked up carrying his small dog which still had no name. "Yes that is good by the Prophet," he said.

Then came five minutes of endless shaking of hands each with the other and each other with each other. It seemed so forced and exaggerated, but it was real.

Then they all started patting the head of the dog as if the dog represented all that was good about life. "That is a good dog you have there, Hakki," said Mahmoud.

"Yes."

"Yes," said Hakki. "Now it is three months old."

"Three months old and still no name?" said Dokki.

"Three months old and still no name," answered Hakki.

"That is no good," said Mahmoud.

Sabra pushed her brother up to the men. Her brother was riding in the green toy car. Sabra stared at the three men without joining in the conversation. She had tried before to think of a name for the dog.

Hakki said that he couldn't think of a name so that he thought it would have to be referred to as The Dog for a good time longer. "Well that is a good enough name for the dog," said Hakki rubbing the puppy's head.

"That is right, Hakki, nothing wrong with calling it The Dog," said Dokki.

***

One of the social problems of Egypt attended to in the immediate period following the death of Nasser was education. This was not because education had been forgotten by Nasser. It certainly had not. But the fact remained that there were many problems due to shortage of teachers, shortage of schools and over supply of graduates in some faculties, which needed attention.

Education always seemed to be the main issue of modern 'revolutions'. Egypt was no exception. In the years following the 1952 revolution, for example, free and compulsory education was introduced for children between the ages of six and twelve. However there was still a great deal of abuse of the system due to the fact that the children were needed to help win the bread for the family, and tend the crops. Although there was a tremendous rise in the number of secondary and primary places offered in schools, attention was not limited to pre-tertiary education level. New universities were opened and existing universities improved.

The Ministry of Education more than doubled its budget in the first twelve years of the revolution and by 1964 it had nearly reached the £100 million level.

However in spite of the tremendous expansion in education there were difficulties. Classes were large due to a great shortage of teachers and schools. There also tended to be an over-emphasis on examinations and lack of imagination in the curricula. In short the faults were those of a production line education in a state that was desperately trying to catch up on what had previously been neglected. This was coupled with the fact that Egypt's population had been rising rapidly providing every year an increasing number of school-age children.

But probably more serious than lack of facilities was the disheartening suffered by the student who having graduated from universities and higher education centres could not find a job. In some sectors of the community the supply of graduates far exceeded the supply of jobs. Whilst in other sectors, for instance medicine and pharmacy, demand for graduates far exceeded the supply.

A study was under way in 1971 to determine the graduate needs of the country. The aim was to strike a balance which was then lacking, between the number of graduates in every branch of specialisation and the actual requirements of Egypt. The Central Organisation for Statistics and Mobilisation had discovered that there was a shortage of graduates trained in pharmacology. There was only one pharmacist for every fourteen thousand people which needless to say was well below the stipulated world minimum.

According to the latest figures in 1971 the number of graduates in Egypt was steadily growing. But even so in the fields where they were really necessary for the developing nation of Egypt they were lacking. Just less than ten thousand doctors graduated between 1960 and 1968 which was two and a half times the number that graduated in the forty-one years prior to the Revolution. However there was still only a ratio of one doctor for every twenty-three hundred people. This was an improvement on 1952 when there was only one doctor for every five thousand people.

Some people argued that there was no longer any need for graduates in such faculties as law, commerce and arts. But according to the Central Organization for Statistics and Mobilisation the demand for graduates in these fields was almost equal to those of the sciences. This seemed questionable.

Another problem was that the very people who were most needed in Egypt seemed to be the ones to emigrate.

To counteract this some restriction was placed on the emigration of doctors and scientists although it was certainly not a blanket restriction. Until 1967 there was almost total restriction on emigration but this was relaxed due to the excessive supply of trained people.

When Dr Fawzi took over as prime minister it was decided that urgent measures had to be taken to repair the failing education system. The measures envisaged included deleting unnecessary subjects at all levels, providing time for extra educational, social and physical activities, reconsideration of the number of compulsory school years, and the offering of meals to school children - a very important factor in a country like Egypt where the people tended to live from day to day.

To enable improvement, Egypt was constantly studying overseas systems, including those of Japan and Russia.

Strangely enough the faults of the system in Egypt were not all due to lack of finance. In many cases it was due to poor teaching methods, badly prepared text books and the fact that there was a high rate of absenteeism, particularly in the country areas where the children were required to help their parents with the crops in the season.

But of course it also suffered from lack of funds like most of the world's education systems. This was even more a problem in Egypt - a country fighting a war against Israel as well as illiteracy.

One had only to walk into any bank or insurance office in Cairo to notice that there were far too many qualified people for the jobs available. Around a table which one imagined was placed for one person, four were sitting. Rooms which were built for two people housed eight or ten. This had also become an argument against automation. In an Egyptian bank where in England one might see a dozen girls working on adding machines, one would see a dozen tables each seating four people all with giant ledgers. Half spent the day asleep on their tables, having literally nothing more interesting than a column of figures to check.

This had led to a great malaise amongst young people who saw nothing in Egypt to look forward to in their career. It didn't suit many to emigrate for obvious personal reasons, but the vision of a lifetime spent adding ledgers did not inspire initiative.

This was probably made worse by the fact that once a person had a job he had it for as long as he wished. Laws prevented the dismissal of workers except in special cases. This meant it did not matter if an employee spent the day achieving little more than the smoking of a packet of cigarettes.

Of course the first to recognise the faults in the Egyptian system were the students themselves. In 1968, they rose in Cairo in demonstration on the excuse of what they considered were lenient sentences passed on air force commanders who had put up a poor display during the Six Day War. But although this was the excuse, they were also against the repressive system as a whole and called for certain reforms including relaxation of the freedom of the press which, incidentally, was becoming more outspoken about the same time. The students also called for a re-organisation of the Arab Socialist Union and the right to form student unions. This last demand was met and Nasser himself agreed to meet student leaders and to hear their complaints.

Dr Fawzi in an interview with Mohammed Heikal published in *Al Ahram* on November 1, 1970 said that the

Egyptian education system could no longer be repaired by patching. It was with this belief that he set his government immediately to work on the task of righting the failing system.

The improvement in education since the revolution had brought tremendous social changes regarding young people, although naturally this was less obvious in the country villages. However there were still inhibitions surrounding the simplest of relationships involving a young man and a young woman. In the mid-sixties it was evidently rare to see two young people walking alone or going out for the evening, but by 1971 this had changed somewhat and was more common. In Cairo streets in the evening though, one more often than not saw a group of young men walking together and further along the street two or three girls walking together, than a young couple. It was even common to see young men walking along hand in hand, or even more daintily, finger in finger. This was certainly not considered unmanly as it might be in London and would certainly be in Australia where men tend not to walk about hand in hand. It further was not uncommon to see young soldiers walking along the Nile corniche on a sunny afternoon hand in hand, although this practice seems to be restricted to non-commissioned ranks.

14. Preparing for new arrivals in Abu el Feda. Sadat woos the masses while tension heightens along the Canal

All was normal in Abu el Feda. Dokki's wife was home again. The sun was shining, but that was normal. Dokki and Mahmoud were exchanging nothings of the mouth. Hakki was pushing and washing cars. Sabra was delivering beer. The hours were passing. Days were also. Life was normal.

This day Dokki was building a fence of cane and wire in preparation for his new baby goat which was to arrive by various calculations within two weeks. Not that anyone knew for certain, but Dokki had been told by a friend the likely time. He had built a small hutch of mud in which he locked the goat at night to protect her from the cold. Pregnant animals are delicate he told his wife. She agreed.

It was lucky that no large block of flats had been built on the land next door as if there had been where on earth could Dokki have put the goats? The land was being put to good use. Dokki had planted onions and beans. That was why the fence was needed, or one of the reasons. It would be no good if the goats, however sweet, ate the vegetables. But the fence was also needed to keep the goats off the busy road.

As Dokki built his fence everyone came to offer advice and enquire the reason for such a strong fence. "It's for the goat when she gives birth," said Dokki.

It was going to be more trouble. With one grown goat tethered to a tree there was nothing to worry about. But a small goat you cannot tether, instead you need a fence.

"That should be a good fence you are building," observed Mahmoud.

"It should be, it has taken him three days to build," commented Sabra.

"I know, I have been watching," admitted Mahmoud.

"Yes it is as strong as strong," said Dokki. "Quite strong enough to withhold a small goat."

"But the mother goat will be able to jump over it, will she not?" questioned Mahmoud.

Dokki took a long look at it and said: "She might, but then I will have her tethered as well."

"Oh, the mother goat will still be tethered?" continued Mahmoud.

Hakki walked across at that stage carrying his puppy. The normal greetings and exaggerated handshakes were exchanged between Hakki and Mahmoud. Then all admired the small dog which had grown to quite a size.

Hakki placed the dog on the ground and walked across to the fence and inspected the workmanship. "That is a good fence you are building, Dokki."

"Thank you Hakki."

"But the goat will be able to jump over it," said Sabra taking up Mahmoud's observation.

"She is right by the Prophet, you won't keep the goat behind that fence, Dokki."

"It is for the small goat when it is born," said Dokki. "The mother goat will still be tethered."

Hakki, Sabra and Mahmoud nodded in understanding.

Suddenly a shriek of brakes came from the road. Of car brakes and tyres skidding on the sun-warmed road was the sound. Then a small thud and a choked scream. Hakki's puppy lay dead before their eyes.

"By the Prophet . . .." cursed Hakki running to his prized possession and lifting it into his arms. But it was still and lifeless, the nameless dog.

The driver of the car stepped from his car. He was confronted with a barrage of abuse. Hakki laid the small puppy at the side of the road and strode across to the man. He put one hand around his neck and was about to punch him on the nose with the other when Dokki restrained him.

None of them had seen exactly what happened. But they were not going to let that prevent them from blaming the man. It was Hakki's dog. It was the man's fault.

A long and involved argument ensued. Hakki asked the man didn't he have any brakes on his car? A question which had been answered by the shriek of the brakes, but nevertheless was worth asking.

"Of course there are brakes on my car," said the man.

"Well why didn't you use them?" said Dokki?

"You have no brakes . . . nor eyes," said Hakki.

"Where is a policeman . . . this car has no brakes," added Mahmoud who had remained quiet until this stage.

Sabra inspected the body of the puppy and a tear began to form in her eye and trickle down her cheek. Her little brother had run off screaming when he had seen what happened.

The argument continued. The man clearly could not make any headway with the argument that the dog ran in front of his car.

"No that is not what happened . . . I saw," said Hakki.

The other two agreed. The man was guilty.

"By God do you repent then?" questioned Hakki.

"Yes, do you repent?" asked Dokki.

"By the Prophet, alright I repent," said the man.

After more discussion the man was allowed to drive off.

The hours passed and the three men considered where the little dog should be buried. They found a plot of ground near the river, dug a grossly inadequate grave and then buried the dog. They then crossed the road and relived the event proclaiming the man guilty.

"The man obviously was not looking where he was driving," said Dokki.

"No . . . must have had his eyes shut," added Hakki.

"Had you thought of a name for the dog, Hakki?" enquired Mahmoud.

"No."

Sabra thought and then said: "Yes, Hakki it will save you giving the dog a name."

Hakki said sadly that he was just thinking what to call it. He added agreement with a false laugh. "Yes, it will save me giving it a name."

The three men shook their heads, more in sadness than anger. Sabra looked up and then said: "Well you can think of a name for our baby goat when it arrives."

"If it is a male you could call it Mohammed," said Hakki. "That is if it will be a Muslim goat."

"The mother is a Muslim, so the child will be born into a Muslim family. A Muslim it will be," said Dokki.

Hakki shrugged his shoulders in a half laugh and then went back to the garage and cleared out the box in which the puppy used to sleep. Then he hosed down the floor getting rid of the last remains of the puppy - its excretions.

***

Just before the end of 1970 Israel agreed to resume contacts with the United Nations mediator, Dr Gunnar Jarring. Mr Riad, Egypt's foreign minister, had been correct in his predictions. Israel's decision was announced just days before the United Nation's Security Council was due to hear a report on the progress made by Dr Jarring's peace mission. Having agreed to resume contacts, Israel fulfilled Mr Riad's other prediction which was that Israel would then press for a further extension of the ceasefire after February 5, 1971.

So the contacts were resumed. What Egypt was now pushing for was real progress towards peace or a settlement before the ceasefire expiry date. It seemed impossible that anything could be achieved in only a month. But Egypt made it her task during January to at least let the world know that nothing was being achieved by peaceful means and that unless Israel's attitude changed she might face another war.

President Sadat was in the position of wanting to make as many war-like noises as possible. The aim of course was to make the Israelis concede something or alternately make their allies, the United States, concede some point to Egypt. The Egyptian President was in the position of having stated categorically that he would not agree to a second extension of the ceasefire period unless real progress had been made under the peace mission of Dr Jarring. Sadat had stipulated that real progress could be in the form of a timetable set for Israeli withdrawal from the occupied Arab territories.

With this aim in mind he committed himself to speak at a number of mass rallies throughout the country. These had the dual purpose of informing the people of the situation and providing an outlet to the world. All these rally speeches were widely reported. At all Sadat received a tumultuous welcome and applause. Although this was partly due to the mass rally atmosphere with cheer leaders and the like, it nevertheless did surprise some observers who had been sceptical all along of Sadat's popularity. Such was the response from the people at these rallies that nobody judging from what he or she saw could ever doubt that the people of Egypt would be prepared to take "other" remedies, meaning military remedies, if diplomacy did not achieve what Egypt wanted. This was exactly what Sadat needed. Had he merely talked to the people from the television it would not have impressed the world that the people were behind Sadat. Also he could not have gone on television telling the people day after day the same thing - which he did at the mass rallies, attended by different audiences.

I remember going to what must have been the most impressive of the rallies. It was at Aswan following the ceremonies marking the completion of the High Dam. Not only were the gathered people addressed by Sadat but also by President Nikolai Podgorny. It was here that Soviet aid in the electrification of Egyptian villages was formally announced to the wild cheers of the people. It was held in a gigantic multi-coloured tent beside a sports ground. Before the speeches began the chanting started. It continually interrupted both leaders especially at any mention of Nasser or Soviet friendship. This rally, like the others, was commenced with readings from the Holy Koran, which one felt had the effect of stimulating the people to receive openly whatever Sadat said. In a sense the rallies, although impressive in their display of support for the new president, were unhealthy in that they contained the manifestations of all public rallies of a nationalistic nature. The people did not consider rationally what was being said, but just accepted it - or so it seemed.

At the time the Egyptian press was taking a pessimistic view of events. Ali Hamdy al Gammal writing in *Al Ahram* put the feeling into words on December 30. "Every decision taken by the Israeli Government indicates beyond any doubt that Israel does not intend to withdraw from the occupied Arab territories, but only endeavours to procrastinate and gain time through an extension of the ceasefire." He went on to point out that after President Sadat's assertion that "we shall not permit any manoeuvre to prolong the occupation of our territories or deny us the right to liberate this territory," it had become clear that events would take a serious turn in the forthcoming days.

Ahmed al Sawy Mohammed writing in *Al Akhbar* pointed out that all indications showed that Israel was not serious in her decision to resume contacts with Dr Jarring. He said that the Egyptian political drive had resulted in isolating Israel and the United States before world public opinion, forcing Israel to declare its resumption of contacts with Jarring, even though this decision was intended merely to procrastinate and prolong the ceasefire.

Then in a move probably aimed at escalating the crisis tension as much as preparing the country for war, President Sadat on December 29 announced mobilisation of the entire home front "to stand on the battle line alongside the armed forces to confront any eventualities during the decisive period of destiny which will face the people after February 5." As part of this mobilisation Sadat asked all political, executive and legislative bodies to place themselves in readiness.

He repeated again that Egypt would not renew the ceasefire for a third period unless serious contacts by Israel had been made towards the implementation of the 1967 United Nations Security Council Resolution, which called for withdrawal of Israel from the occupied territories.

As a means of mobilisation he stipulated that every governorate was to become an integrated independent unit which would directly shoulder the responsibilities as far as preparedness was concerned. Every governorate was to have a command committee which would lead the work required to be carried out. This mainly comprised existing officials: the governor, governorate secretary of the Arab Socialist Union, the head of the regional group at the National Assembly, the Director of Security for the area, and the military advisor of the governorate. War committees were also to be formed at village level to handle all matters concerned with the mobilisation. Probably speaking from past experiences the President added that full cooperation was required among all political, executive and legislative agencies and that there could be no excuses or lagging on the part of any of the officials.

He then gave his account of the events since the Six Day War up until the present time. He alleged that Israel had escalated the crisis in December 1969 by using 264 planes in a raid on Egyptian positions from morning until late afternoon. He said that when this failed to bring about the desired effect, Israel had moved into the second stage by extending its raids to Tel el Kebir and Inshass. "The main purpose," said the Egyptian president "was to demonstrate Israel's full command of our air space and destroy our air defence system."

He said the third stage of escalation by Israel commenced in January 1970 when she raided the Abu Zaabal factory. The strategy of the enemy during the first half of 1970 was directed against the internal front. But this, he said, only increased the people's determination to resist. Nasser had made a little-publicised trip to Moscow late in January 1970 and agreement was reached to supply Egypt with the SAM 3 batteries. A notable exception in Sadat's survey of the history of the crisis escalation was Nasser's War of Attrition which lasted up until the ceasefire was declared in August 1970.

The following day *Al Ahram* commented editorially on Israel's decision to resume contacts with Dr Gunnar Jarring. It questioned: "Is it a genuine resumption of contacts or is it a mere manoeuvre by which Israel aims at gaining time and avoiding a report by U Thant condemning Israel for obstructing peaceful endeavours to solve the crisis?"

The same day President Sadat visited the front and spent nine hours with the armed forces' commanders. He evidently told the army that the Egyptian people had absolute confidence in them and fully appreciated their efforts.

The atmosphere at this time was yes, Israel had agreed to resume peace contacts, but no, nothing would come out of them at least before the expiry of the ceasefire. As far as the Egyptian Government was concerned this was not going to enable them to extend the ceasefire on their previously stated terms.

Al Ahram, commenting on Sadat's mobilisation of the home front said: "Preparedness for all eventualities including a decisive battle, is the responsibility of each citizen. No one among us should pretend or imagine that he had no place in the battle and that he has no duty towards it, or to say that it is not the responsibility of the armed forces."

In spite of all these rousing words it appeared that no change was really taking place in the outlook of the Egyptian people at this stage. February 5 after all, and the possible decisive battle, were a month away.

Prior to addressing Egyptian newsmen on January 2, President Sadat discussed with Egypt's chief delegate to the Jarring talks, Dr Mohammed Hassan el Zayyat, the stand to be taken at the resumed contacts in New York. Dr Zayyat left Cairo two days later for New York. Dr Zayyat himself was showing pessimism about the resumed Jarring mission. He said: "Israel has so far continued to challenge the United Nations. But now she tries to change the picture by showing readiness to contact Jarring and then blaming the Arabs for failure of the talks. It is clear that the resolution passed by the U.N. General Assembly which requested U Thant to present a report on Jarring's contacts was the reason which made Israel contact Jarring."

The Egyptian delegate had spent the past days conferring with Mr Riad, Egyptian Foreign Minister, and other senior officials on the stand to be taken at the resumed talks.

Dr Zayyat said then that his contacts with Jarring would be based on two principles. Firstly Egypt's refusal to surrender to Israel's will and secondly, his country's acceptance of the Resolutions passed by the U.N. General Assembly and the Security Council and her readiness to carry them out.

According to *Al Ahram*, Sadat had received a comprehensive report on Egyptian-Soviet relations following the talks held in Moscow between the two countries. A considerable part of the report was said to be devoted to the results reached by the joint military committee, and the "full understanding" of the Egyptian military requirements demonstrated by the Soviet side. Perhaps it was little coincidence that this was leaked in the semi-official press just two days prior to Dr Zayyat's contacts with Jarring. Some saw this as a thinly veiled threat to Israel that should the Jarring talks not be carried on in earnest, Egypt would be ready militarily with the continued support of the Soviet Union.

Commenting on the situation, *Al Ahram* said that the Israeli procrastination, fully backed by the United States, would only result in further complication of the situation for which Israel and the United States would be held responsible.

The meeting with senior Egyptian newsmen, or as Cairo radio described them, "men of thought", was the first of the series of speeches Sadat was to deliver in the month preceding the ceasefire expiry date. The others were to the mass rallies. The most notable thing to come out of this address was the mention of a small number of Russians who had been killed whilst manning missiles. This although contradictory in that Sadat had said that Egyptians were in control of the defence of the country, did seem to indicate that at least some Russians were involved in the missile air defence system, a fact which had always been assumed but never admitted publicly. Although this statement was made by the President himself, it was censored from all but one dispatch by foreign correspondents from Cairo. It seemed that no significance could be placed on the fact that one dispatch did get through, it was probably due purely to the haphazard censorship in Egypt.

Sadat said that the armed forces had not wasted a moment of the ceasefire period making use of it in reinforcing their positions. Then came the contradiction: "Egyptians are themselves manning all the weapons." He did not however say whether only Egyptians were manning all the weapons.

"We have commanders for all types of modern warfare including an electronic war. It pleases me and honours me to say that all personnel in charge of this work are Egyptians who have completed their training with an efficiency that has surprised even the Russians themselves." If it was so it would have also surprised several observers who had always believed that Russians commanded the SAM 3 sites. However the wording of the President's statement did leave open the possibility that Russians were merely advising the Egyptian commanders.

Then Sadat drew his distinction between the relationship between Israel and the United States and the Egyptian-Russian relationship. "Israel considers itself the first line of defence of the United States' imperialistic interests in the area while relations between us and the Soviet Union are based on a joint objective, namely to combat imperialism and achieve peace based on justice." Some people would perhaps not see such a distinction in the two relationships, but then Sadat could not after all be placed in a category of unbiased observers of the Middle East. He noted that the first batch of SAM 3 missile batteries had been installed within the span of forty days at the cost of one million pounds per day.

On January 4 President Sadat was due to attend the first mass rally, the second speech in the proposed series. *Al Ahram* commented on the importance of these addresses. Editorially it said: "The meetings which President Sadat is holding with the various sections of the people acquire special importance for they come in circumstances when the battle of the Arab nation is moving through an extremely serious phase. Now either the Security Council Resolution is implemented and the Israeli forces withdrawn from the occupied Arab territories, or the ceasefire will not be binding anymore."

The second speech by President Sadat, this time to fifteen thousand people in the provincial city of Tanta dealt more with the war which seemed inevitable than the peace moves which might avoid it. Parts of the speech were Churchillian in flavour: "The coming war will be total and the United Arab Republic has no alternative but to plunge into it and pay any price. This war would not be only at the battlefront but will be fought everywhere - in villages, fields, factories and streets." While stating that Egypt had become strong economically, militarily and politically, he noted that Israel was still strong, but that "we shall fight the battle whatever the cost and price." He added to the loud applause of the people that the ceasefire would not be extended a second time unless Israel set a definite timetable for withdrawal from the occupied territories. This was what "real progress" entailed.

On January 5 the report by Dr Jarring to the United Nations Security Council was made public. Israel had already resumed contacts as Egypt had predicted so it was not as damning as it might have been, however it still made it clear that Israel had hindered progress of the peace mission. Although the sixteen page report included only the official messages exchanged between Jarring and the three countries concerned, it did give a picture of a gloomy situation.

Answers to questions put to the three countries in March 1969 were included in the report. Jarring had asked Egypt, Jordan and Israel to define their stands on the Security Council Resolution of November 22 1967, how they believed a just and permanent peace could be brought about, and how the problem of the Palestinian refugees could be settled. Replying, Egypt and Jordan declared their readiness to carry out the resolution ending the state of war when all Israeli troops were withdrawn from the occupied territories. However, Israel had pointed out that secure and recognised borders had never existed between her and the Arab states. Israel added that accordingly they should be established as part of the peace-making process. In answer to a question whether she would withdraw from the territories occupied in 1967, Israel replied that when permanent, secure and recognised boundaries were determined in the peace treaty, withdrawal would be to these. Regarding the Palestinian refugees, Israel had called for a conference of the Middle East countries to work out a five year plan to integrate the refugees into productive life. Presumably Israel meant productive life in the Arab countries as well as in Israel.

The same day as the report was published, Dr Zayyat, Egypt's delegate to the peace mission, said following his first meeting with Dr Jarring since contacts had been resumed that he felt less optimistic and that the Israelis were impeding progress towards the implementation of the 1967 Resolution. Commenting on reports that Israel had invited Jarring to visit Tel Aviv as what the Egyptian press described as "part of her manoeuvres which aim at obstructing his mission," Dr Zayyat said: "I do not want to be a party to manoeuvres designed to delay the mission and therefore I did not propose that Jarring should visit Cairo."

At the same time Mr Riad was in London as part of Egypt's mammoth diplomatic campaign. He asked Britain in her capacity as one of the Big Four powers to work for the implementation of the 1967 Resolution. Egypt had been encouraged by an apparent shift in Britain's policy towards the Arabs.

The same day and less encouraging to the Egyptians were President Nixon's statements at a press conference expressing the United States' readiness to continue supplying Israel with arms. Nixon had said that the U.S. would continue to maintain the balance of power in the Middle East.

Commenting on the resumed Jarring contacts and Egypt's belief that Israel was merely delaying matters to enable the ceasefire to be extended along the present borders, *Al Ahram* wrote: "Israel had not resumed contacts with Gunnar Jarring when it became clear that her intention was to continue her policy of procrastination and foot-dragging and preventing any serious start to the implementation of the Security Council Resolution. This was revealed by a statement Israeli delegate to the United Nations, Joseph Tekoah, made in Tel Aviv before leaving for New York. Tekoah summed up the Israeli policy when he said that the first round of talks would be confined to procedural matters and that he did not expect that any discussion would take place concerning the matter of the Middle East crisis before three months. What was important for the time being, Tekoah added, was to maintain the ceasefire."

Israeli Defence Minister Moshe Dayan told the Knesset on January 6 that Egypt had installed about one hundred ground-to-air SAM 2 and SAM 3 missile batteries in an area extending 50 kilometres west of the Suez Canal. He said that one third of these were of the SAM 3 variety which were effective against low-flying aircraft. He added that Egypt had also deployed 250 heavy and medium artillery guns in front positions.

The following day news agencies in Israel were quoting unnamed Israeli "sources" as saying that Egyptian troops were streaming into the canal front with equipment for crossing and the most modern missiles including ground-to-ground missiles. Israeli military "circles" were quoted as saying that the number of Egyptian troops stationed along the canal was estimated at six armoured divisions equipped with about six hundred tanks. The Israeli reports went on to say that the possibility of a major crossing operation by the Egyptians was not excluded.

There was in fact a build-up of Egyptian military power along the Suez Canal about this time, but it was not nearly as sudden as these reports would have had one believe. There was perhaps a bit of truth in both the Israeli and Egyptian views of the situation. Israeli sources were stating that Egyptian troop concentrations were aimed at pressuring Israel into accepting a timetable for withdrawal. The Egyptians were saying that Israel's statements were aimed at turning public opinion away from Egypt at the time of resumed contacts and also to continue the flow of arms from the U.S. to Israel under the "pretence" of balancing power in the area.

In the next of his programmed speeches President Sadat said on January 8 that the problem for Egypt was not Israel, but America. He repeated his allegation that the U.S. was merely using the excuse of balance of power to enable more arms to be sent to Israel. He stressed that the ceasefire could not under the present circumstances be extended again. Although this speech was continuing the line of no further ceasefire, it was gentler in its outlook. In a sense it was a turning point and concentrated on peace rather than war as a solution.

Meanwhile Dr Jarring had made his trip to Israel. America had pointed out that this balanced the advantage Egypt had achieved when Mr Riad had seen Dr Jarring in Moscow during Riad's visit with the delegation led by Egyptian Vice President Aly Sabry. During this visit Dr

Jarring was in Moscow continuing his task as Swedish ambassador to the Russian capital. However Egypt was not pleased with the fact that Dr Jarring was venturing personally to the Middle East. Israel all along wanted the talks to be held firstly, directly between Egyptian and Israeli leaders, and secondly on neutral ground nearer to the Middle East situation, probably Cyprus. They objected to the contacts being held in New York. On the other hand, Egypt supported the New York venue because it was an excellent stage from which to bargain, her plan so much depending upon the sympathy of the world which could easily be rallied at the U.N. where she had many more supporters than Israel. Egyptian leaders at no time invited Dr Jarring to visit Cairo because they felt this would open up the possibility of contacts being held away from New York. So in the event Jarring returned to New York and the contacts were resumed at delegate level.

On January 10 President Sadat, addressing academics in the provincial city of Asyut, reiterated that Egypt would not extend the ceasefire for a single hour unless a timetable was set for Israeli withdrawal. "This," he said, "is the only solution ahead of us involving more pains and more sacrifices, but I do not have the slightest doubt that we will win the battle if we pay the price."

President Sadat denied an allegation made both in Israel and the United States that Egypt's rejection of a further extension of the ceasefire after February 5, 1971, amounted to a declaration of war. He said that these allegations were aimed at influencing world opinion against Egypt. The Egyptian view was that although they would not extend the ceasefire they would not necessarily start shooting immediately, if at all.

The Egyptian President also spoke of the facilities - water and some food - Egypt was giving Russian naval ships which used Alexandria harbour. When the facilities were arranged by Nasser, an envoy of President Johnson, according to Sadat, had warned the late president of the perils of communism. Sadat said Nasser told the envoy: "Tell Johnson thank you but don't worry about us. We want no tutelage. Tell him the facilities will not only be for water but for provisions as well. They stood by us in the dark hours and we want no advice from anybody."

The following day, addressing a mass rally in Asyut, President Sadat attacked the United States saying that America had brought pressure to bear on Egypt following the death of Nasser in the hope that the internal front would collapse. Sadat said the United States insisted on treating Egypt as a defeated people who had to accept conditions imposed on the vanquished. "I declare to America that we lost the battle but not the war." The withdrawal timetable condition of ceasefire extension was repeated in this speech.

At the mass rally held on January 15 marking the completion of the High Dam Sadat repeated most of the points he had been making with regard to extension of the ceasefire, but the most important aspect of this mass rally was the disclosure by President Podgorny that Russia would help with the electrification of the Egyptian villages. Following this rally and up to a few days before the ceasefire was due to expire all remained fairly dormant in Cairo. Although it was assumed that all the same conditions for ceasefire extension remained, nobody said so very loudly.

During this period the second major summit meeting between the four Arab countries which had agreed to work towards federation was held in Cairo. It was in fact the first that Syria had attended. At the end of the summit the leaders President Sadat, Libya's Colonel Gaddafy, Sudanese President Nimeiry, and Syria's Hafez el Assad issued a joint communiqué, but this dealt generally with the crisis, condemned Zionism and the U.S., supported the Palestinian cause, and stated that the whole Arab potential would be mobilised behind the causes.

15. Winter ends in Luxor. Preparing for war in Cairo

Hassan noticed the hot sun on his back. It must be the end of winter, he thought. Time to move from Luxor to Cairo it was. In Cairo the winter lasted longer. Best to get there and make use of the last respite from the hot sun before the summer swamped the whole of the country. All these years, all these summers, but one never seemed to get used to it, he thought.

It was for that reason that Hassan was standing beside the railway line in Luxor. He was waiting for the next train to Cairo. Dusk had just fallen and the train should have been along in about half an hour. Hassan always found that whenever he had to catch a train he was always early. He always ended up waiting some time for it. And so often the train was late also which made his wait all the longer. Better to be safe though, he thought. He was waiting just on the Cairo side of the station. The train would come from Aswan, come into the station, stop to pick up the paying passengers, and then move off again. It was then that Hassan was going to make his move. Before the train picked up too much speed he was going to leap up the steps at the front of the engine and then scramble on to the roof.

No one else was waiting this night, so he just stood there thinking. Thinking of the winter: the most pleasant winter in Luxor. It really paid its way, he reckoned. Better and better conditions, it was a wonder more people did not do it. But it would be good to get back to Cairo;

back to Abu el Feda. A breeze had come up and he felt a little cold. The days were hot, but the nights still cold.

At last the headlights of the train could be seen in the distance. Hassan looked directly at it squinting. Like a black monster approaching out of the night. All he could make out was the light. As the train made its way into the station, the driver, dressed in khaki army-style uniform waved to his friends on the platform. It was a bit as if he was running a lap of honour after a sub-four minute mile. He was a hero. Plenty of people would willingly drive the great monster down the Egyptian lifeline. Like everyone else in Egypt the driver and his assistant had a good supply of Turkish coffee ready for the trip. The train stopped.

Hassan stood watching the proceedings. Watching the people get on and the people get off. All finished, the train honked the horn and slowly began to move. The time for which Hassan had been waiting. He fixed his eyes on the steps leading on to the engine. Just at the right moment he stepped up. That was it. Much easier to do it when there were no other people there tripping you up, he thought as he clambered on to the top of the train. The engine was quite warm which was good to combat the night breeze.

He settled down, putting his head on his shining rag and his box of polishes between his legs not noticing the dark form also on the engine.

"Hello friend," came a voice.

Hassan looked up with a start and said: "Hello friend, I did not see you."

"Going Cairo?" questioned the voice.

"Yes . . . have you come all the way from Aswan?"

"Yes all the way by the Prophet, all the way."

The two talked for a time and then both lay down on the jolting train trying to get some sleep. How on earth they did not fall off no-one would ever know. Hassan lay there thinking . . . Thinking of Cairo . . . Thinking of Luxor . . . Thinking of the long night ahead.

***

In the week before the ceasefire was due to expire on February 5, 1971 there were reports from both sides of the canal of intensive military preparations and "high tension" along the fighting fronts. In Cairo there had been civilian preparations taken. The headlights of all cars had to be painted blue and windows of buildings shuttered in preparation for the possible "decisive battle" following the elapse of the ceasefire. Mock air raids were held throughout the country to test the readiness of the people.

The painting blue of car headlights must at a conservative estimate have given hundreds of otherwise unemployed small boys a job for as long as the emergency lasted, which in the event was less than a week. These little boys equipped with an old jam tin full of blue paint would stand at one of the many intersections in Cairo where traffic was delayed for periods up to half an hour. Here while one was trapped in an inescapable jam they would ask whether you wanted your lights painted blue. One was an open target because obviously if they were not already painted you should get them painted to abide by the law. However I, not I think because I was too mean to pay the two piaster price but rather because I wanted to use a paint that could later be washed off, refused. But the little boy went ahead and lavishly covered the headlights with blue paint - or so it seemed. Then he came up although I had not wanted it done and asked for just one piaster. I refused. My meanness was rewarded when I returned home to find the lights as they had always been. The boy had not painted them at all.

On January 30 Israel lodged her thirty-third complaint with the U.N. Truce Supervision Organisation against alleged Egyptian violations of the ceasefire. Israel alleged that two Egyptian fighter-bombers had flown over Israeli positions on the eastern bank of the Suez Canal. Egypt did not deny the charge.

All through the week there were frantic diplomatic efforts in world capitals attempting to persuade Egypt to extend the ceasefire. However Egypt was giving the appearance of sticking to her pledge that there would be no extension unless real progress had been achieved in the Jarring contacts.

However on February 2, 1971 U Thant, the U.N. Secretary General, in a report to the Security Council on the Jarring contacts appealed to the parties concerned to maintain self-restraint and to maintain the calm that had prevailed in the area since August 1970, the month the ceasefire came into effect. He also said that although the resumed contacts were still at an early stage and much further clarification was required, he found grounds for "cautious optimism" in the fact that the parties had resumed contacts in a serious manner and that there had been some progress in the definition of their positions. At no stage did he appeal to Egypt to formally extend the ceasefire, but merely appealed for self-restraint and maintenance of the calm. This was obviously done to leave Sadat to extend unofficially the ceasefire if he felt that he could not, without losing face, do so formally. Egypt's delegate to the Jarring contacts, Dr Zayyat, commenting on U Thant's report, said he did not share the feeling of "cautious optimism."

The same day Egypt's National Defence Council, the country's highest strategic planning body, met under President Sadat. In this meeting just three days before the ceasefire was due to lapse, the decision was made to extend it for a further thirty days. However nothing was made public at this stage.

This same day Israel lodged her thirty-fifth complaint against Egypt alleging overflying across her positions along the canal.

It was not until the night of February 4, just hours before the ceasefire was due to end that the Egyptian decision was announced. In an eleventh hour address Sadat told Egypt's National Assembly that during this thirty day extension Israel must make real progress towards peace through the United Nations mediator Dr Gunnar Jarring. President Sadat said real peace depended upon the withdrawal of Israel from occupied Arab lands. He said liberation of all the lands occupied after the Six Day War in 1967 was Egypt's aim. United Nations Secretary General U Thant was asked to make a full report on the progress of the Jarring Mission before the thirty day extension expired.

President Sadat called upon Israel to withdraw at least partially her troops from the Suez Canal zone during the thirty day extension. He said that if Israeli troops were withdrawn from the eastern bank of the canal, Egypt would then be immediately prepared to clear the canal for international shipping.

The Egyptian President stressed that Egypt had always pursued every possibility of peace and this extension was merely a continuation of this policy. "We have performed our duties towards the world with the utmost effort and endeavour and it is time when others should assume their responsibilities towards the world and towards peace," said Sadat.

In the speech, broadcast live over Cairo radio, President Sadat said the extension had been agreed following a request by U Thant and several nations sympathetic to the Arab cause that no fighting should take place. He pointed out that Egypt had agreed to the extension despite the fact that she believed no progress had been made so far by the Jarring Mission towards the implementation of the 1967 United Nations Resolution calling for the withdrawal of Israel from the occupied territories.

16. New arrivals in Abu el Feda. The extended ceasefire and Israel's reaction to Egypt's proposal for withdrawal from the Canal

It was all happening. Dokki's goat was producing. All were watching. It was not a secluded birth. Sabra, Sami, Mahmoud, Hakki and Dokki were supervising. Hassan was offering to clean the shoes of the spectators whilst they watched the greatest show in Abu el Feda for a long time. Not that they could really see anything. For the mud hutch Dokki had built made sure of that. But every now and then Dokki would step forward, quietly poke his head in the entrance, and give a progress report.

Hassan had arrived back just that morning. So was slightly put out that his return was not the big event of the day. But then that was the way things went. Things were unpredictably predictable. Arrive back the same morning Dokki's goat is producing and you cannot expect much attention, thought Hassan philosophically.

He cleaned Hakki's shoes. But Hakki thought he should pay nothing since Hassan should be glad to be back. But things did not work that way and he reluctantly handed over two piasters. Then Hassan brushed Dokki's shoes. But this was often interrupted by Dokki taking a look at his goat.

"Good, very good," said Dokki as he looked into the hutch.

Good very good mightn't mean a lot literally, but it meant a lot to the spectators. It was as if they all knew what stage the birth was at.

"Good, very good," said Dokki again. All was going well.

It was a sunny day. It was good to be back, thought Hassan. Not as hot as in Luxor, but nevertheless sunny . . . very pleasant. Then came the news.

"That is good," said Dokki. It was over. Another goat had entered the world.

"By the Prophet," said Mahmoud who had delayed gas deliveries especially for the event.

"By the Prophet," joined in Hakki.

"Is it a boy or a girl?" questioned Sabra.

"I can't tell," said Dokki.

"Well we cannot give it a name yet then," commented Sabra.

The hours passed, and much to the surprise of all, everything did not seem to be over in the goat hutch. The goat, not satisfied with the one offspring it had already produced, seemed to be commencing the procedure again. It was to Dokki's delight. Hassan could not waste his time just looking so had gone his way looking for custom, but he was back every now and then for progress reports. Hakki also had to leave to push a car or wash down the garage floor. Most things went on as usual although it was a special day. But Dokki maintained a permanent vigil outside the hutch. He was accompanied by Sami and Sabra, who were spending the time thinking of names, both male and female because Dokki had not yet discovered the sex of the first arrival.

"Mohammed if it is a boy," said Sabra.

"And what if it is a girl?" questioned Sami.

The answer was not forthcoming. What on earth can you call a female goat?

Then broke the silent thought.

"By the Prophet," said Dokki. At Dokki's words all assembled. All gathered to hear the news. Yes, another goat had been born.

"Is it a boy or a girl?" questioned Sabra. But Dokki did not know.

"By the Prophet," said Hassan who had returned just in time for the event. "By the Prophet Dokki, you are a lucky man."

"A lucky man?" And then Dokki added: "A lucky man, yes I am by the Prophet."

The scene returned to normal, or nearly. But something strange was happening in the hutch.

"It is almost as if she has not finished yet, by the Prophet," said Dokki.

"Has not finished?" questioned Hassan.

"Dokki is thinking wishfully," commented Hakki.

"I suppose so," said Dokki.

"You should be satisfied with what you have already got," said Hassan.

"I am satisfied," said Dokki. "But take a look in the hutch for yourself..."

Hakki and Hassan and Mahmoud who had just ridden up again on his tricycle with a new batch of gas, moved cautiously towards the entrance of the hutch. They took a look inside.

"By the Prophet," said the three in unison.

"I think you are right," said Hassan.

"It looks that way," commented Hakki.

Mahmoud just stood looking in stunned amazement. Two already and a third on the way; is that possible? The next hour was spent chewing over this question. Everyone had a cup of Turkish coffee, or as some of the more nationalistic people in Egypt would say, Egyptian coffee. Then what they had cautiously predicted happened.

"By the Prophet, it is so. Another goat," announced Dokki. The others shook their heads in wonderment. Sabra was too amazed to question again the sex. Hakki just looked at Dokki: this morning a goat owner, this afternoon a farmer.

***

So Egypt had agreed to an extension of the ceasefire. For thirty days at least there would still be no fighting. By extending the ceasefire for only thirty days President Sadat had bowed to world opinion - even won some new friends, but had not relieved the Middle East of the tension Egypt so badly needed to maintain. If the extension had been for another three months nothing diplomatically may have been attempted, let alone achieved, until the second month was over. But with only thirty days Israel was obliged to at least reply to Sadat's suggestion of a partial withdrawal to enable reopening of the canal for world shipping.

Some immediate Israeli reactions rejected the Egyptian idea out of hand, but obviously they caused some embarrassment later. Embarrassment not because they did not express the opinion of the Israeli Government, but because they were open and not what was needed to prolong the diplomatic talk which kept Israel's borders at the post-Six Day War positions. Egypt had undoubtedly been cunning. Most, if not all seafaring countries of the world - and many others as well - would welcome the re-opening of the canal.

On February 7, the Israeli Cabinet met and considered Sadat's speech. The meeting was more than usually secret and evidently all members of the cabinet were instructed not to make statements. The meeting was extended and included the Chief of Staff, General Barlev and other senior officers. They decided to seek clarification from Dr Jarring on the Egyptian initiative.

On February 9, Mrs Golda Meir, the Israeli prime minister, made a statement to the Knesset. She expressed the view that the Egyptian Government's decision to withhold fire for thirty days was an ultimatum to resume fighting on March 7, 1971. She said that Israel was nevertheless called upon to continue contacts with Dr Jarring under threat of this ultimatum. Mrs Meir said she was prepared to talk separately about re-opening the Suez Canal, but only provided it was re-opened to all ships including those flying the Israeli flag. She said that such talks might also include the cutting down of military preparations on both sides of the waterway prior to the normalisation of civilian life in the canal area.

An official Egyptian spokesman immediately stated: "The United Arab Republic considers that Mrs Golda Meir's statement is a flat rejection of the Egyptian peace initiative and that it reaffirms Israel's persistence in imposing its terms on the Arabs. Mrs Meir talked much about peace and her desire for peace at a time when all the acts of Israel spell out action against peace."

Al Ahram, commenting editorially after noting Mrs Meir's statement as a rejection of the Egyptian initiative, said: "It also implies the attempt to use this initiative to continue the Israeli policy of shunning contacts with Jarring by isolating any step that could be a starting point for the implementation of the Security Council Resolution and withdrawal from the occupied territories." The following day February 10, Mr Abba Eban, the Israeli foreign minister, said that Israel believed progress towards peace was conditional upon the implementation of two points. Firstly the abolition of the deadline of the ceasefire along the canal which now was to expire on March 7. It should instead be extended indefinitely. Secondly, discussion about the re-opening of the Suez Canal for international shipping should include reference to ships flying the Israeli flag. As Egyptians noted however, he made no mention of Israeli withdrawal, partial or otherwise. He was asked whether Israel would withdraw from Jarring's contacts if Egypt opened fire following the expiry of the ceasefire period. He replied: "If the U.A.R. opens fire, we will say the U.A.R. has withdrawn from the Jarring contacts."

American Secretary of State Mr William Rogers said the same day that he was encouraged by Mrs Meir's statement, which he said showed Israel's interest in following Egypt's proposal for re-opening the canal. He said it left the door open for further discussion. The Egyptian press however, saw Rogers' statement as merely aimed at persuading public opinion that Meir's statement was hopeful.

Commented Aly Hamdy al Gammal in *Al Ahram*: "It has now become evident to everybody that Israel does not want peace, and is keen on maintaining the state of war because she gains by making the world believe that she lives in permanent danger. We have said our last and final word. And since Israel, with the support of America, imagines that she can continue the occupation of the Arab territories, then we have no alternative but to liberate our lands with armed force."

Then as insults continued to be aimed at opposite sides of the canal, Dr Gunnar Jarring came up with a new plan. He sent a two page questionnaire to Egypt, Jordan and Israel asking them what they considered would satisfy each in a peace deal. In effect he was asking them to state categorically what they wanted; what their terms were.

When the new Jarring proposals arrived in Cairo, Egypt could almost have been described as sharing the "cautious optimism" expressed by U Thant, U.N. Secretary General, before the thirty day ceasefire extension had been agreed by President Sadat.

Following meetings between Egypt's foreign minister, Mr Mahmoud Riad, and Sir Richard Beaumont, the British ambassador in Cairo, and the ambassadors of France and Russia as well as with the head of the American interests section in Egypt, President Sadat and Dr Fawzi the prime minister, met and considered the Jarring proposals. These in part stipulated withdrawal from the occupied Arab territories. Then the full Egyptian cabinet met and further considered the proposals. The Egyptians were being unusually quiet about the exact content of the proposals by Jarring but this silence was taken as an indication of their optimism. The New York correspondent of *Al Ahram* described the proposals as a "positive move".

Under Jarring's new proposals it seemed at the time that Israel would be required to withdraw from the occupied Egyptian territories including the Gaza strip and Sharm el Sheikh commanding the Straits of Tiran. However, a supervision force of some kind was envisaged at Sharm el Sheikh to ensure Israel's access to the port of Eilat at the far end of the Gulf of Aqaba.

Except for the request for concrete demands from the three parties which could form the basis of a negotiated peace, Jarring's proposals did not seem to be very much different from the demands of the 1967 United Nations Resolution calling for Israeli withdrawal from the occupied territories, hence Egypt's optimism and Israel's disinterest with the proposals.

The Israeli reaction was not diplomatic. Like so many recent Israeli statements it appeared unconsidered and hasty. Mrs Meir suggested that the methods followed by Dr Jarring constituted a departure from the norms of world diplomacy. Her deputy Yigal Allon commented that Dr Jarring was not an arbitrator and he was not in a position to put forward proposals. The immediate Israeli reaction was in short that Jarring had overstepped his task. However a blow to this view came when United States Assistant Secretary of State, Joseph Sisco said in a television interview that the United States Government had full confidence in Dr Jarring and said that he was working well within his powers.

Then an interview with President Sadat published in *Newsweek* clarified some points regarding the "partial withdrawal" Sadat had mentioned in his speech extending the ceasefire. He said in answer to questions by *Newsweek*'s Arnaud de Borchgrave that this meant withdrawal to a line behind El Arish. Only a quick glance at a map will show anyone why observers were surprised that this was described by Sadat as merely "partial withdrawal". It also became apparent that Egypt was prepared to sign a peace treaty with Israel, the one thing the Israeli State had always wanted more than anything. It would mean recognition of borders by the dominant Arab state. More significant still was Sadat's reply to a question regarding the Palestinian refugees. The question was: "There is still much confusion about the Palestinian problem. What would be your objection to adequate financial compensation for Palestinian refugees coupled with a referendum in the West Bank and Gaza to determine whether Palestinians want a separate state, either federated or confederated with Jordan, or to remain an integral part of Jordan?" The reply was: "I'm not in a position to decide for the Palestinians but this sounds a reasonable way to solve the problem - compensation and referendum. They must decide for themselves."

In the version of the interview published internally in Egypt, this reply was omitted together with several other replies. The internal version gave a considerably harder view of Sadat's demands than the actual *Newsweek* version. Enquiring at the Middle East News Agency, which distributed the internal version, I ascertained that their report came direct from the Presidency. They could not say whether it had in fact been censored. Evidently what happened was that during the interview the Presidency tape-recorded, or at least recorded, the dialogue and then made their own transcript for distribution without referring to *Newsweek*'s version. I asked the Presidency to comment on whether they had purposely censored the transcript to give a harsher impression to the people at home of Sadat's demands. I did not ever get a reply, but in Egypt that could not be taken necessarily as an admission of guilt.

Epilogue

Having already backed down once on his pledge that an extension of the ceasefire depended upon real progress being made by the Jarring Mission, Sadat was clearly in a corner when the thirty day ceasefire expired on March 7, 1971. When extending the ceasefire on February 4 he had stated that although he believed no real progress had been achieved, he would agree to a further extension for one month.

The case was different before the March 7 expiry. Jarring clearly had not achieved anything real - or at least nothing real enough to enable Sadat to tell the people of Egypt that his condition had been achieved and that he was now able to extend the ceasefire for a further period. He had no alternative than to lapse the ceasefire. But at the same time he declared that Egypt would not initiate any fighting along the front with Israel. Although not formally, the ceasefire was still in effect.

It was a stalemate. Little seemed to have been achieved during the seven months of ceasefire, but at least nothing had been destroyed. The parties did not seem to be progressing along the road to peace, but at least they were not retreating. And this in the drawn-out crisis in the Middle East was something. Nasser was dead and some people were quite wrongly noting that Sadat was behaving more reasonably than his predecessor. But this completely ignored the fact that it was one of Nasser's last acts to accept the Rogers' plan and the ceasefire - surely the turning point in Egypt's attitude if there was one. Nasser was dead, but Egypt was uncannily strong, militarily, but more importantly, diplomatically. Rumblings from Washington were putting pressure on Israel to at least be a little more temperate and work towards peace. But the situation remained the same: Israel holding her battle-won lands and Egypt demanding them back. Both were threatening war as an alternative to peaceful diplomatic negotiation, but neither wanted to follow that course. It was a stalemate.

***

Life in Abu el Feda progressed as usual. Dokki's new goats were a month old and all three were well. Dokki had fed them a pile of green grass he and Sabra had collected from the river bank, and was now sitting on his seat beside the road. He was watching the passing scene.

Hassan was on the other side of the road surveying the scene from his eyes stationed at the top of that long, aquiline nose. Watching to see if there were any possible shoes in need of shining, but there were none. The sun was on his back and he felt tired as he watched the scene he had watched so many times before. He saw Hakki washing a car, Sabra delivering beer and every now and then Mahmoud riding past delivering gas.

The hours passed and as the sun fell in the sky he made his way across the road towards Dokki. He asked if he could leave his box of shining equipment under the staircase for the night. Dokki refused and then after long and involved deliberation agreed to Hassan's request.

"By the Prophet, I will clean your shoes tomorrow for no charge," Hassan told Dokki.

"By the Prophet you will too," said Dokki as he waved a farewell to Hassan.

Hassan made his way up the street, galabia flowing in the evening breeze. The end of another day.

The End.

www.ingramcontent.com/pod-product-compliance
Lightning Source LLC
LaVergne TN
LVHW091254080426
835510LV00007B/255